OUT OF THIS WORLD

Southern Poets

Edited by Vicki Skelton

First published in Great Britain in 2015 by:
Young Writers
Remus House
Coltsfoot Drive
Peterborough
PE2 9BF
Telephone: 01733 890066
Website: www.youngwriters.co.uk

Book Design by Ashley Janson

SB ISBN 978-1-78443-432-8

Printed and bound in the UK by BookPrintingUK
Website: www.bookprintinguk.com

FOREWORD

Here at Young Writers our defining aim is to promote the joys of reading and writing to children and young adults and we are committed to nurturing the creative talents of the next generation. By allowing them to see their own work in print we believe their confidence and love of creative writing will grow.

Out Of This World is our latest fantastic competition, specifically designed to encourage the writing skills of primary school children through the medium of poetry. From the high quality of entries received, it is clear that it really captured the imagination of all involved.

We are proud to present the resulting collection of poems that we are sure will amuse and inspire.

An absorbing insight into the imagination and thoughts of the young, we hope you will agree that this fantastic anthology is one to delight the whole family again and again.

CONTENTS

Sophie Hopkins (9) 1
Neha Vijayakumar (10) 2
Joshua Powell-Laide (9) 3
Hareesha Uthayasekaran 3
Georgina Powell-Laide (7) 4
Kyla Hayward (9) 4
Dahlia Davis (7) 5

Ashill Community Primary School, Ilminster

Libby T 5
Josh T 5
Bevan W (8) 6
Zoe C (8) 6

Bathampton Primary School, Bath

Arthur McGuinness (8) 6
Erin Hart & Pelagia Beekma (9) 7
Mia Hart (9) 7
Harry Sinclair (8) 8
Stanley Cope (8) 8
Bertie Lye (8) 9
Amelie Penman (8) 9
Maria Maylor (8) 10
Charlie Hedges (8) 10
Olivia Corry (8) 11
Cameron Skipp (8) 11
Isaac Parry (8) 12
Isabel Da Cunha Beesley (8) 12
Eric Bathurst (8) 13
Sophie Ball (8) 13
Gabriel Adams-Wainwright (8) 13
Genie Murray (8) 14
Toby Wright (8) 14
Sky Hodgson (8) 15
Alberto Trent (8) 15
Billy Nash (8) 16

Farleigh School, Andover

Lucas Gardner (10) 16

FKS Schools, Dunmow

Joshua Bryan (8) 17
Giosué Calleja (8) 18
Victoria Smith (8) 18
Olivia Gravatt (8) 19
Mehar Bhatnagar (8) 19
Charlie Murphy (9) 20
Hossein Habibpour (9) 20
Finley Homer (8) 21
Caitlin Abercromby (8) 21
Charlie Bywater (8) 22
Georgia Ward (8) 22
William Frost (8) 23
Jessica Carmichael (9) 23
Ted Reeves (8) 24

Four Lanes Infant School, Basingstoke

Oliver Cavill (7) 24
Jessica Hoile (7) 25
Aiden Kennedy 25
Lillia Chilton-Bull (6) 26
Aminah Imran (6) 26
Libby Eves (6) 27
Rhys Harrison (6) 27
Amelia Walton (6) 28
Freya James 28
Rebecca Hoile (7) 29
Emily Mansbridge (7) 29
Eliana Buckley (7) 30
Hannah Vincze (6) 30
Amrit Gahir (6) 31
Jack Girling (7) 31
Ashton Vivian (6) 32
Sophia Sarsby (6) 32
Lauren Radley (7) 33
Kieran Woodhead (6) 33
Emily Hogan (6) 34
Tahlia Gani (7) 34
Fredrik Eason (6) 34
Erin Daniel (7) 35
Kimberley Chapman (6) 35
Lucy Pilbeam (6) 35

Elizabeth Cowley (6)................................ 36
Blandine Thiebauld (6) 36
Ty Minikin (6) 36
Joshua Vaughan (7) 37
Ben Chambers (7) 37
Faye Concannon (6)................................ 37
Arun Tatter (6).. 38
Harry Randall... 38
Yehia Alsaedi (6)..................................... 38
Freddie Cox (6).. 39
Steven Webb (6)...................................... 39
Emmy Harfield (6).................................... 39
Sam Goldsmith (7).................................. 40
Zach Roff (7)... 40
Harry Rolfe (6) 40
Alicia Goacher (6).................................... 41
Phoebe Read (6) 41
Isla Doe (6).. 41
Poppy Johns (7) 42
Amy Phillips (7)....................................... 42
Alex Morley (6) 42
William Robins (6) 43
Airon Martin (6)....................................... 43
Henry Wheeler (6) 43
Dylan Mortimer (7).................................. 43

Kent College Junior School, Canterbury

Anna Silver (10)...................................... 44

Kitebrook House, Moreton-In-Marsh

Lily Radford (10) 44
Sophia McAlpine (9) 45
Max Craig (7)... 45
Loelia Bailey (9)...................................... 46
Barnaby Coldridge................................... 46
Miller Sherwood (9) 47
Lucy Tibbitts (10) 47
Jasper Brumpton (9)................................ 48
Noah Kirkham (10) 48
Chloe Fermor (9) 49
Sophie Marsden (10) 49
Imogen Shackleton (10) 50
Ophelia Clarke (10) 50
Imogen Brumpton (11)............................ 51
Henry Austin (10)..................................... 51
William Cecil (7)...................................... 52
Theo Peake (7).. 52
Cecilia Loudon (8) 53
Bob Rawlinson (8) 53
Oliver Riley (8)... 54
Tabitha Moore (9) 54
Mason Chambers (7).............................. 55
Charlotte Mackinnon (8) 55
Paige-Allen Thomas (7).......................... 56
William Noble (7) 56
Deven Trotman (7).................................. 56
Tabitha Little (8) 57
Mark Jonsson 57
Alice Hannah (8)..................................... 58
Scrase Duffy (10).................................... 58
Emily Szor (8) 58

Leweston Junior School, Sherborne

Issy Colwell (11) 59
Eve Fidler 60
Annabel Bruller (10)................................ 60

St John's CE School, Salisbury

Kiara Holley-Paliano (6).......................... 61
Oliver Bowden 61
Nicole Roberts (6).................................. 61
Ruby Dicker.. 62
Daisy Baker 62
Reo Ridout (5) 62
Chloe Hall.. 63
Felix King... 63

St Peter's CE School, Aylesford

Rubyleigh Emery (10)............................. 63
Hannah Burton (10) 64
Hannah Sparks (7) 64
Isla Trotter (7) 65
Gabi Goemans (7) 65
Sophie Matthews (7)............................... 66
Aiden Clark (8)... 66
Emily Champion (7) 67
Amber Gower (8)..................................... 67
Brooke Gillingham (7)............................. 67
Lily Viner (9) 68
Jack Neal (6) 68
Jodie Leigh Leigh Harris (7) 68

Telscombe Cliffs Primary School, Peacehaven

Jalani Odle (6) 69
Yzabella Liezl Demaisip (6) 69
Monty Capildeo (6) 70
Stanley Webb (7) 70
Isla Young (6) 71
Sienna Price (6) 71
Jake Baldey 71
Lucy Renshaw (7) 72
Kaitlin Cork (6) 72
James Barrow (6) 72
Max Hughes (6) 73
Phoenix Rogers (6) 73

The James Oglethorpe Primary School, Upminster

Harrison Bradbury (8) 73
Enrike Kukulskis (8) 74
Madison Golding (7) 74
Oscar Corbett (7) 75
Kyle Hewson (9) 75
Tilly Ott (8) 76
Niamh Shelley (8) 76
Grace Tyler (8) 77
Jack Sanderson (7) 77
Neve Willcocks (8) 78
Ben Stokes (8) 78
Olivia Thomas (8) 79
Anjolaoluwa Adeniji (7) 79
Jacob Cornwell (8) 80
Isobel Davies (8) 80
Jessica Rogers (9) 81
Christina SadikaJ (8) 81
Louis Geater (7) 81
Millicent Murray (8) 82
Archie Powell (7) 82
Ruby Elsdon (8) 82
Dylan Teece (7) 83
Chloe Taylor (8) 83
Georgia Phillipson (8) 83
Brandon Phillips (9) 84
Jude Butler (9) 84
Mia Sweeney (9) 84
Joshua Hobbs (8) 85
Glen Wiggins (8) 85
George Seaman (9) 85
Kyla Dixson (8) 85
Noah Smith (7) 86
Katie Waller (8) 86
Zoë Roberts (7) 86
Rebecca Francs (8) 87
Jayma Thomas (8) 87
William Jones (8) 87
Tillie Callis (7) 88
Tyler Robertson (9) 88
Lexie Ive & Jada Nnodim (8) 88
Emma Chambers (8) 89

Westbury On Trym CE Academy, Bristol

Amy Parkin (11) 89
Florence Spear (10) 90
Olivia King (10) 90
Lily Randhawa (10) 91
Megan Saunders (11) 91
David McGregor (10) 92
Rabia Hassan (10) 92
Oliver Vowles (10) 93
Ben Beggs (10) 93

Woodside Primary School, Ruardean Woodside

Azura Elizabeth Smith 94
Ella Kear (7) 94
Jeremy Maxwell 95
Jacob Wragg-Jones 95
Demi Harbinson (7) 96
Jayden Jones 96
Neo Gardiner 97
Bobby Potter-Thomas 97
Thomas Hamm 98
Callum Alexander Johnston (7) 98
Kyran Peter Jack Meek (8) 98

Yeading Junior School, Hayes

Samragyi Pokhrel (9) 99
Shivleen Gill (10) 100
Zaim Abdin (10) 101
Tia Sanghani (10) 102
Akshayian Ganesharatanam (9) 102
Drishtee Sookraj (9) 103
Mikaiel Shuaib (10) 103
Balraj Singh Virdi (9) 104

Jasmin Kaur Sidhu-Bansal 104
Ahees Thevarajah (9) 105
Vigash Tharamavarthan 105
Shuceyb Moalim (9) 106
Nisha Saroye 106
Rayaan Ahmed (9) 107
Gurshan Basra 107
Harnimrat Sidhu 108
Muteen Ali-Choudhrey (10) 108
Sukhmani Hayre (9) 109
Sopna Shanmugathas (9) 109
Roshan Kundi (9) 110
Vaishnavi Namanather (9) 110
Neil Sorthia (9) 111
Heba Agal (7) 111
Sopisa Mohanachselvan (9) 112
Yaqub Hassan (9) 112
Bhavika Athiparan (7) 113
Fakeha Mirza (10) 113
Nishanjit Tamber (9) 114
Aaliyah Cumberbatch (9) 114
Mariam Abdilahi (9) 115
Riya Valji 115
Sagana Baskar (9) 116
Kiran Saroye (8) 116
Hannan Ahmed (10) 117
Asvin Srimurgan (9) 117
Yonathan Aklilu (7) 118
Gajuri Thevarajah (7) 118
Banujas Siva (7) 119
Ayaan Jelle (9) 119
Angelina Ali Pestana (10) 120
Fatema Mirza (7) 120
Ally Mohammed (10) 120
Ilma Gouse (7) 121
Nemat Malik (7) 121
Mohammed Ali (7) 121

THE POEMS

My Garden

My garden is a comfortable place,
Bright green leaves tickle your face.
Blood-red roses burst from tiny shoots,
The cherry tree and her roots.
The emerald-green grass sways in the breeze,
The branches of the many trees.
The delicate flowers that spring from the ground,
Spots of colour, dotted around.
In autumn, the leaves fall in a flurry,
Red, brown, gold and green, dancing, not in a hurry.
Winter comes by with a layer of frost,
It is a beauty that does not cost.
Spring shoots up to answer Mother Nature's cry,
Then summer comes with herbs under an azure sky.
The sun shines upon the grass,
It is a moment that will pass,
Not without a moment's thought,
Here is something that can't be bought.
The dew that sparkles in the sun,
The slides, the trampoline that's fun.
Walk slowly down the patio stair,
The garden laid before you, beloved care.
The messy bushes and flourishing trees,
The lavender fragrant for the buzzy bees.
The common blackbirds that come to sing,
As sublime, in my eyes, as anything.
The predatory cats stalk my robin red,
It flutters away, turning its little head.
The place that lies beyond my back door,
I learn to love it more and more.

Sophie Hopkins (9)

Hot . . .

The grievous heat scalding my back,
Causing my neck to leisurely crack.
The boiling sun bids to blind me,
In East Africa where I be.
Ambling through the withering crops,
Sauntering along the obsolete docks,
Its a monstrous feat with parching heat,
In East Africa where I be.
The sun is emerging majestically like a crimson orb in the sky,
And shattering all our ambition and gain,
And causing life to die.
The trees no more waltz under the watch of the sky,
The vines are no more showing an array of tangles and ties.
The flowers would show a display of vermilion, gold and green,
But they have now ceased blooming it seems,
Heat caresses the land with a blazing scorching touch,
Setting the horizon ablaze and demolishing much.
The air ripples with melancholy and woe,
Our residents plead for the sweltering heat to go.
Our fate is undoubtedly unknown to all,
With its heat the sinister sun challenges us to a brawl.
Death will rise
And warmth will come,
Our blithe thoughts will become glum.
Our faces scarlet from our working pace,
As drops of sweat trickle down our helpless face.
We are here no more, who am I writing this for?
Life is perished here,
Starvation is near.

Neha Vijayakumar (10)

What Am I?

Ten-headed
Square-faced
Extra-strong
Magic-drainers
Jelly-bellies
Eight-legged
Laser-users
Shape-shifters
Mind-readers
Carrot-eaters
Really-big
Bumpy-skin
Super-fast
Very-slimy
High-flyers
Always thinking
Rocket-makers
Tech-lovers
Satellite-stealers
I'm an . . . alien.

Joshua Powell-Laide (9)

The Storm

One shivering storm,
It looked like hailstones were falling down the path,
The path was very swampy and soggy.
Raindrops tapped on the window lightly at first,
And then drummed on the roof angrily,
Creating a frightening loud noise.
The blizzard damaged many buildings,
People's homes had electricity cuts.
There was a crash of thunder,
And a strike of lightning went past.

Hareesha Uthayasekaran

Awesome Aliens

Aliens, oh amazing aliens
Stinky feet
Cheesy treat
Yummy to eat

Aliens, oh silly aliens
Big ears
Purple eyes
Streaming tears

Aliens, oh perfect aliens
Spotty face
Spiky back
Ten eyes come out of his head

Aliens, oh amazing aliens
Blue arms
White, perfect teeth
Stinky feet.

Georgina Powell-Laide (7)

My Pets

I have a Yorkshire terrier called Lilly
And sometimes she can be a bit silly.
An American bulldog called Diesel,
That is full of fuel and lots of energy.
I have a cat called Samsung.
He doesn't know how to work a phone or a TV.
I have a hamster called Harry
That runs around my bedroom in a hurry.
One goldfish called Barbie
That loves to party!

Kyla Hayward (9)

Christmas

This poem is about something
That everybody looks forward to every day,
It's Christmas where your parents dress us
As Santa and everybody celebrates by singing carols
And unwrapping presents.
What Christmas is all about
Is spending time together.

Dahlia Davis (7)

Winter - Haiku

The fluttering snow
Falling slowly on the lake
Deep snow on the hill.

Libby T
Ashill Community Primary School, Ilminster

Autumn - Haiku

Red leaves on the trees
Falling down in the calm breeze
Rustling as you step.

Josh T
Ashill Community Primary School, Ilminster

Autumn - Haiku

Leaves falling like bats
Prickly hedgehogs are snuffling
Lovely crunchy leaves.

Bevan W (8)
Ashill Community Primary School, Ilminster

Rain

Storm clouds look like grey pillows that are about to rain.
Rain is giants' teardrops.

Zoe C (8)
Ashill Community Primary School, Ilminster

While I Watch Weather

The sky was as dark as a black panther
Creeping through the grass.

The wind whispered as softly,
As softly as someone blowing.

Rapidly the raindrops poured down
Like loads of people throwing water around.

The thunder was as loud
As people banging saucepans together.

The fog was as thick
As an elephant's leg.

It was as bright
As people flickering lights on and off.

Arthur McGuinness (8)
Bathampton Primary School, Bath

Sundrops And Snowdrops

When you hear a grr
You might see a quick orange flash.

Watch out the sun is gazing at you.
Even at night-time you see a sunbeam as red as could be.

In the blizzard far away you feel a frostbite coming.
Snow trickles down as you jump around.

In your home you're so snug,
Outside the animals hug.

Feel the snow crispy cold
Even when you have your gloves.

Even when snow is melting
Keep that frown upside down.

Erin Hart & Pelagia Beekma (9)
Bathampton Primary School, Bath

Winter

Winter is cold,
Summer is hot,
There was once a green tree in summer
But white in windy winter.
A flicker of light,
A snowflake floats down
To its ice palace.
The orange and yellow
Comes out at daytime
And night-time!
Winter is as cold as a cucumber.
Summer is as dry as a bone.
Thank winter for the soft snow.
Thank summer for the super sun.

Mia Hart (9)
Bathampton Primary School, Bath

Snow Rays

On a sunny day
The snow comes through a ray,
In the middle of May,
The boiling sun blares snow,
In piles.

The sunrays as cold as ice,
The drops as small mice,
Spinning like a dice,
The snow as fluffy as a bear,
Falling as quick as a hare,
As cold as icicles.

Harry Sinclair (8)
Bathampton Primary School, Bath

Weather Workers

Thunder roaring like a silver buck warning its herd.
Thunder roaring, swiftly falling.
Clouds drifting like whales in a pod,
Roaring quite odd.
Rain sparkling like diamonds.
Snow swiftly falling to its ice palace.
Wind could be as light as a feather
Yet could be as strong as a hammer.
Rain giving life to Earth.
Weather working together to make people happy.

Stanley Cope (8)
Bathampton Primary School, Bath

Stormy Saturday

Suddenly the sky went dark,
Everything was quiet,
Except for the kettle boiling,
It was as gloomy as a basement,
I was as scared as a mouse,
About to be pounced on,
Out of nowhere roaring lightning hit my fence,
Then it hit it again,
Finally it stopped and skipped away,
But the rain rained as wild as a bear.

Bertie Lye (8)
Bathampton Primary School, Bath

Snowflake

S now is as white as a wedding dress.
N ever as hot as hot chocolate
O h no here comes the snow
W eather is falling fast like snow
F rosting the warm water
L ooking at the poor cold people in the freezing snow
A mazingly the white snow stays so long
K icking poor snowmen over
E ventually it melts away.

Amelie Penman (8)
Bathampton Primary School, Bath

A Teddy Bear On A Stormy Night

It was a dark and stormy night,
A teddy bear was all cuddled up in his bed.
The thunder was as loud as a lion's roar,
It was as frightening as a horror movie.

Whilst the raging storm was going on outside,
The teddy bear was all nice and warm.
Tucked up in bed,
In his heated house.

Maria Maylor (8)
Bathampton Primary School, Bath

Sunflakes

On a sunny day
The sun comes down in flakes.
Everybody cries as they watch the sunny lakes.
The sunny flakes are as hot as a volcano,
They beat down on houses
And come through the chimney.
They come down like snowflakes,
They look like boiling orange drops.

Charlie Hedges (8)
Bathampton Primary School, Bath

Weather

W eather is falling like snowflakes off a house chimney
E lectric lightning strikes a beautiful house
A ll the water rains like a deep blue ocean falling from the sky slowly
T hundering thunder scaring a charming cheetah
H undreds of snowflakes falling down onto a spiky bush
E aster rain is very gentle like a hamster in a hamster ball
R emember December is my birthday.

Olivia Corry (8)
Bathampton Primary School, Bath

Stormy Night

The sky went as dark as the middle of the night
Like mid-December in a power cut
The wind whispered as soft as a mouse
Pouncing like the leaves being blown about.
Rapidly raindrops fell
Like tears falling down a crying baby's cheek in a tantrum.
Then there was thunder as loud as a plane
Crashing onto a nearby hill.

Cameron Skipp (8)
Bathampton Primary School, Bath

Animal In The Elements

The lion roared as loud as thunder.
The white wolf as white as snow.
The skin of a rhino as hard as hail.
The whale as wet as rain itself.
The elephant stampede as loud as the wind.
A lion's mane as soft as a cloud.
The sky is as blue as the fish.
A dark cloud as dark as a crow.

Isaac Parry (8)
Bathampton Primary School, Bath

Stormy Night

The sky went as dark as a gloomy, pitch-black, old cellar,
As dark as space,
The sky went as dark as a huge light switching off.
The wind whispered as quietly as a mouse creeping
Into a whole piece of cheese.
Rapidly raindrops fell
From the heavy sky to the street
Like rushing, racing cars on a race track.

Isabel Da Cunha Beesley (8)
Bathampton Primary School, Bath

October Owl

It's October now
The leaves are falling
The owls are ready for winter migration
One of the owls is sitting on the vast oak
Leaves are falling on the owl
The leaves look like clouds, some even look like stars.

Eric Bathurst (8)
Bathampton Primary School, Bath

Sunflakes

The sunflakes amazingly amused the children,
They fall from the sky,
They are lovely things that dance in the sky,
But if you go too close to them,
They pop in your face
And that is the end of that.

Sophie Ball (8)
Bathampton Primary School, Bath

Rain And Snow

Rain and snow,
Rain and snow.
Cold and wet
like the winter crew.
Super cold and super wet
But I bet you'll get wet.

Gabriel Adams-Wainwright (8)
Bathampton Primary School, Bath

Stormy Night

The sky went as dark as a shady tree
In the middle of the night
As dark as a deep, dark black cave
The wind whispered like a mouse squeaking
Rapidly raindrops fell like rushing and rolling rivers
Down a steep mountainside.

Genie Murray (8)
Bathampton Primary School, Bath

Stormy Night

The sky was as black as a bat.
The sky was as dark as a big bat cave.
The wind whispered as softly as a rabbit hopping.
The thunder was as loud as a dragon breathing fire
Banging, booming, bashing.

Toby Wright (8)
Bathampton Primary School, Bath

Stormy Night

Rapidly raindrops fell loudly onto the ground
Like rolling rivers, making a pitter-patter sound.
The sky went as dark as a black bat,
Asleep in a deep, dark cave,
Then there was thunder as loud as a lion roaring.

Sky Hodgson (8)
Bathampton Primary School, Bath

Untitled

The sky went as dark as a deep dark cave.
The wind whispered as quietly as a barn owl
Flying over the fields.
The raindrops fell rapidly
Like hailstones falling down.

Alberto Trent (8)
Bathampton Primary School, Bath

Weather Warrior

The rain patted down like arrows hitting the ground.
A man retreated as fast as stormy wind.
We went down as slow as the most gentle breeze.
When we were down we landed like autumn leaves.

Billy Nash (8)
Bathampton Primary School, Bath

Out Of This World

I love this sport,
Riding mini tidal waves
Bigger than you can even imagine,
Make one mistake
And you're dead!
Only the most experienced can do it,
It is breathtaking to watch
But terrifying to do,
To ride a maverick
Is truly out of this world!

Lucas Gardner (10)
Farleigh School, Andover

A Scary War

I was walking around with my gun, I thought I was the last man alive
When the others started shouting, to get away I had to dive.
I was running for my life
Because they were chasing me down with a knife.
When I finally got away
I met a wounded man on my way.
I still had some medicine from the hospital.
A man started shooting with his pistol.
I shot back with my gun.
I heard a tank,
A man was shouting, 'Incoming.'
I quickly crawled onto the land
And I found a man who had no hand.
Then I realised I was in a bad place.
I ran away with him on my shoulder.
Oh no, we can't get through, there's a boulder.
The enemies came crashing in.
We were surrounded.
I thought about my gun,
I got it out and bang, we had won.

Joshua Bryan (8)
FKS Schools, Dunmow

Invasion

Bombs fall
Bullets are fired
Planes fly
Soldiers and paratroopers die
Crafts land
On the sand
Shells explode
Ships turn to firing mode
Torpedoes strike
Veterans start the long dangerous hike
Up the mountains forts prepare
No man will be spared
Please God shut the door
On all the horrors of war!

Giosué Calleja (8)
FKS Schools, Dunmow

Pets, Pets, Pets!

'I want a pet,' said Lily to her mother.
'No, no, Lily, not another!
You've got two dogs, a cat with six kittens,
Hamsters, guinea pigs and a horse with three mittens.

A budgie, a squirrel, a flock of sheep,
Really Lily, none of this was cheap.'
'But it's not one of those Mum, honest I don't lie,
They don't even cost as much as a pie.

We might need a net,
We might get wet.
For all I want are some tadpoles Mother!'

Victoria Smith (8)
FKS Schools, Dunmow

Halloween/Mum's Birthday

On Halloween it's my mum's birthday,
That makes it an extra special day.
First we decorate the cakes
That my nana always bakes.
Then there's the costumes!
I used to be a cat
And then I'm a bat.
Now I'm a witch
I'm never going to switch.
Finally Mum blows out the candles,
As she jingles her new bangles.

Olivia Gravatt (8)
FKS Schools, Dunmow

Halloween

Children dressed up spookily as wizards.
Children go knocking on doors
Searching for sweets.
They gobble their sweets greedily.
They eat sweets louder than five mes!
Children yell, 'Trick or treat?'
While hoping Halloween will never end
From bed I can hear yelling.
Ah, what a noise!
The children go home, unable to finish their sweets.
The next minute they're snoring loudly on the floor.

Mehar Bhatnagar (8)
FKS Schools, Dunmow

Dinosaurs

Dinosaurs are scary, some are not,
Some live in cold places, some live in hot,
The T-rex has teeth that are bigger than me
And it will always win the fight, as you will see,
Some eat grass and leaves,
They wouldn't harm a swarm of bees,
If you go back there now, you'd be squashed,
Because all their big feet go *bish, bash, bosh,*
If you were there they'd rip you apart,
But luckily they're fossils so we're not in that part.

Charlie Murphy (9)
FKS Schools, Dunmow

The Robot Dog

He ran to Dan quickly,
Luckily he ate his food.
He stole my keys
As he was a Dalmatian.
He was sick
As he had an infection.

He barks,
He heard a cat,
He saw a herd of sheep.

Hossein Habibpour (9)
FKS Schools, Dunmow

Halloween

The spooky lights shine on the street,
As everyone is trick or treating,
In the distance I see a vampire eating sweets
While he knocks on doors and screams, 'Trick or treat?'
I see pumpkins glowing orange on the window sill
As I hide behind the bush,
While the street lights beam on me
The people give me nightmares.

Finley Homer (8)
FKS Schools, Dunmow

Winter

The icy breeze
Makes the icicles freeze
The buzzard howls like a wolf
And the cold creeps up your face
It is freezing cold so wrap up warm
And when you go in go near the fire.

Caitlin Abercromby (8)
FKS Schools, Dunmow

My Puppy

My puppy is hyper
Her tail flaps
She plays with a fly
She lays on the bed then flies by
After flying off the bed she flies towards the couch
I think she's rather silly
Now it's bedtime she pounces on the bed
And curls up nice and tight and says goodnight.

Charlie Bywater (8)
FKS Schools, Dunmow

Halloween

The dressing up is extreme
The sweets are all delicious and scrumptious
The dark and scary night is so spooky
Maybe there are witches and wizards out there
Maybe there are werewolves and ghosts
The best bit for me is making my parents spends loads of money
And of course the sweets!

Georgia Ward (8)
FKS Schools, Dunmow

World War Two

In my trench, in my terror,
Lies ahead a German,
In a bang, in a screech,
Here comes the MG reach,
While we charge,
Men flop down with blood in all directions,
After this war poppies grow everywhere.

William Frost (8)
FKS Schools, Dunmow

My Five Days Of Living

On day one I learnt to talk,
Then on day two I started to walk,
When day three came I made a phone call,
But on day four I threw a ball at my mum,
So then on day five I died in a fire fight
And that is how I'm up here with you.

Jessica Carmichael (9)
FKS Schools, Dunmow

The Forest

The snow shines and glistens
As the sun rises over the horizon
Water starts falling all around me
As ice starts melting and snow begins to fall
All around me is thick white snow and light blue ice.

Ted Reeves (8)
FKS Schools, Dunmow

In The Castle

I listened to shiny swords clashing loudly
In the light green grass of the battlefield.
I saw a glimpse of a tribe of brown rats scuttling quickly
In the big, posh and grand kitchen.
I felt rough cobblestone and the mossy floor in the extremely big courtyard.
I sampled juicy, fruity, cold water
And roasted chicken in the posh, big and grand dinning room.
I sniffed at the smell of bread baking, that was wafting through the grand hallway.

Oliver Cavill (7)
Four Lanes Infant School, Basingstoke

In The Castle

I heard some jolly music playing in the big ballroom.
I saw a beautiful, sparkly crown as bright as sunshine locked in a tall, brick tower.
I stroked a big, black, friendly horse standing in its wooden, brown, big stable.
I tasted a scrumptious bowl of yummy vegetable soup cooking over the burning hot fire.
I smelt a scrumptious roast chicken laid out on a yummy banquet.

Jessica Hoile (7)
Four Lanes Infant School, Basingstoke

A Knight For The Day

I listened to armour rattling noisily
On the extremely sweaty soldiers at the rocky battlefield.
I glimmered at a posh princess prancing elegantly in the fancy ballroom.
I licked a couple of juicy slices of baked chicken in the busy kitchen.
I sniffed some steamy smoke swirling slowly at the top of the brick chimney pot.
I felt some shiny rubies on the pointy crown in the huge crown room.

Aiden Kennedy
Four Lanes Infant School, Basingstoke

In The Castle

I heard swans splashing loudly in the shiny, sparkly and wet moat.
I noticed the queen snoozing quietly in her posh, beautiful bedroom.
I touched the powerful, cute horses cautiously in the dirty stables.
I tasted the brown, hot roast chicken hungrily waiting in the hot dining room for me.
I smelled the king's hot chocolate waiting in the dining room to be drunk.

Lillia Chilton-Bull (6)
Four Lanes Infant School, Basingstoke

The Castle

I smelled a spreading wafting smoke in the gigantic drawing room.
I gobbled apples, juicy grapes and bananas quickly in the king's room.
I spotted a knight training carefully in the green, muddy and huge battlefield.
I noticed the cook sleeping happily in the smelly kitchen.
I stroked soft and cosy mattresses in the queen's beautiful bedroom.

Aminah Imran (6)
Four Lanes Infant School, Basingstoke

In The Castle

I listen to a dragon roaring as loud as thunder in the big dragon courtyard.
I spotted a gorgeous princess dancing merrily in the huge ballroom.
I stroked the pretty princess' ginger and white cat in the short princess' own huge bedroom.
I tasted a scrumptious banquet in the pretty garden.
I smelt the queen's pretty perfume outside the big royal gate.

Libby Eves (6)
Four Lanes Infant School, Basingstoke

In The Castle

I saw the important queen hanging her beautiful dresses in the dusty cupboard.
I touched a juicy roast chicken carefully in the busy kitchen.
I heard water splashing noisily in the glimmering moat.
I tasted scrumptious, juicy roast chicken quickly in the sumptuous dining room.
I sniffed some delicious food bubbling quietly in the castle kitchen.

Rhys Harrison (6)
Four Lanes Infant School, Basingstoke

Senses

I glanced at a golden crown shimmering brightly in the posh throne room.
I smelled a fine loaf of soft white bread baking in the hot kitchen.
I felt the grassy and sandy floor of the battlefield curiously.
I tasted some juicy roast chicken hungrily in the sumptuous dining room.
I heard the annoying chef singing untunefully in the royal kitchen.

Amelia Walton (6)
Four Lanes Infant School, Basingstoke

In The Castle

I touched a very shiny coat of arms so I touched it very carefully.
I tasted a delicious, scrumptious roast chicken
So I ate two bites because it was so delicious and scrumptious.
I saw the queen's corgi running past and it looked cute.
I heard a grey, scary, evil wolf howling in the dark, spooky, gloomy woods.
I smelt a delicious roast chicken in the big, big dungeon.

Freya James
Four Lanes Infant School, Basingstoke

Untitled

I slurped the king's hot chocolate hungrily
Which was waiting to be eaten in the posh dining room.
I sniffed the white, soft bread cooking slowly in the hot oven.
I listened to the soldiers marching noisily on the front path.
I spotted the fierce knights fighting bravely in the damp, dark field.
I felt the diamonds carefully that were on the sparkly crown in the red throne room.

Rebecca Hoile (7)
Four Lanes Infant School, Basingstoke

In The Castle

I heard a powerful witch chuckling loudly in the dangerous room.
I glanced at a pretty, kind-hearted princess singing gorgeously in her huge bedroom.
I stroked a black and white furry kitten
Who was purring softly on the fluffy couch in the big living room.
I tasted a lovely, delicious banquet in the dining room.
I smelled a chicken roasting in the clean kitchen.

Emily Mansbridge (7)
Four Lanes Infant School, Basingstoke

In The Castle

In the castle
I heard a green dragon roaring in the enchanted forest.
I noticed a beautiful princess dancing gracefully in the huge ball room.
I stroked the little corgi lying in the hallway.
I tasted a yummy banquet in the enormous garden.
I sniffed the fragrant flowers on the table in the great hall.

Eliana Buckley (7)
Four Lanes Infant School, Basingstoke

In The Castle

I heard the noisy pots bubbling loudly in the dirty kitchen.
I saw the queen's fancy, sparkling and beautiful dresses
Hanging smartly in the big wooden cupboard.
I felt the mossy walls carefully in the damp dungeon.
I tasted the king's yummy hot chocolate sneakily in the quiet dining room.
I smelled the dirty rats racing in the dark dungeon.

Hannah Vincze (6)
Four Lanes Infant School, Basingstoke

In The Castle

I saw the queen's cute corgis running madly in the lovely hallway.
I heard rats scuttling quickly in the spooky, gloomy and scary dungeon.
I stroked beautiful swans swimming gracefully in the shimmering blue pond.
I tasted a piece of steak hungrily in the fancy, lovely dining room.
I smelled a scrumptious banquet in the beautiful, colourful kitchen.

Amrit Gahir (6)
Four Lanes Infant School, Basingstoke

The Five Senses

I saw the king's sparkly crown shimmering in the grand castle crown room.
I tasted some lovely juicy chicken slowly in the bustling kitchen.
I touched the mossy cobblestones carefully in the twisting pathways.
I heard swords clashing loudly in the giant courtyard.
I smelled thick smoke wafting through the pathways coming from the cold, damp dungeon.

Jack Girling (7)
Four Lanes Infant School, Basingstoke

In The Castle

I heard smart soldiers marching quickly in the big courtyard.
I saw an owl flying quickly outside in the sun.
I touched a soft dress hanging smartly in the sumptuous dressing room.
I tasted a juicy and sweet roast chicken waiting to be eaten in the clean kitchen.
I smelled the king's hot chocolate in the clean dining room.

Ashton Vivian (6)
Four Lanes Infant School, Basingstoke

In The Castle

I felt the very soft cushions lying on the royal sofa.
I tasted scrumptious roast chicken on the grand plate.
I smelt a disgusting poisonous potion that was made by the evil cook in the kitchen.
I heard a powerful king shouting on his diamond throne.
I spotted a beautiful princess dancing in the hallway.

Sophia Sarsby (6)
Four Lanes Infant School, Basingstoke

Dazzle

I saw a dazzling dress hanging smartly in the huge cupboard.
I heard children speaking loudly in the bedroom.
I touched smooth horses carefully in their stables.
I tasted some juicy roast chicken popping quietly in the kitchen.
I smelled some of the king's hot chocolate bubbling loudly in the bedroom.

Lauren Radley (7)
Four Lanes Infant School, Basingstoke

In The Castle

In the castle . . . I saw noisy swords clashing loudly in the green, big battlefield.
I heard disgusting rats scuttling quickly in the massive corridor.
I touched a delicate crown in the small crown room.
I tasted a fat roasted chicken in the gigantic kitchen.
I smelled disgusting socks in the brown wardrobe.

Kieran Woodhead (6)
Four Lanes Infant School, Basingstoke

My Senses

I heard the black rats scuttling loudly in the stony corridors.
I saw a sparkly and golden crown shining brightly in the sparkling crown room.
I touched fluffy black horses carefully in the dirty hay stable.
I tasted roast chicken in the giant kitchen.
I smelled bread baking in the cosy kitchen.

Emily Hogan (6)
Four Lanes Infant School, Basingstoke

In The Castle

I heard a silver wolf howling in the dark forest.
I saw a wicked witch cooking a bubbling potion in the gloomy dungeon.
I touched a black cat sitting on the small wall in the royal garden.
I tasted a delicious banquet in the clean kitchen.
I smelled the queen's flower perfume from her big bedroom.

Tahlia Gani (7)
Four Lanes Infant School, Basingstoke

In The Castle

I heard the fast-flowing moat in the dark, gloomy forest.
I saw a knight with armour so bright that you cannot look at it in the enchanted forest.
I touched a ginger cat in the magical throne room.
I tasted champagne at the delicious banquet.
I smelled dirty washing in the washing machine.

Fredrik Eason (6)
Four Lanes Infant School, Basingstoke

Untitled

In the castle
I heard a hot fire roaring in the huge ballroom.
I saw a glamorous princess dancing in the enchanted forest.
I touched the golden orb and sceptre in the queen's royal cupboard.
I tasted the juicy steak in the big dining room.
I smelled tasty beef on the clean white cloth.

Erin Daniel (7)
Four Lanes Infant School, Basingstoke

In The Castle

I heard a cute bird whistling in a healthy tree.
I saw a colourful big flag flapping in the strong wind on top of the tallest turret.
I touched the brave knight's silver armour in the long hall.
I ate a yummy honey cake in the smelly kitchen.
I smelt a scrumptious chocolate cake in the big dining room.

Kimberley Chapman (6)
Four Lanes Infant School, Basingstoke

In The Castle

I heard the soldiers marching noisily in the wide battlefield.
I saw the happy queen's corgis running madly in the smelly courtyard.
I touched a shiny, white vase gently in the gorgeous crown room.
I tasted a juicy piece of chicken noisily in the big dining room.
I smelled roast potatoes cooking quickly in the posh kitchen.

Lucy Pilbeam (6)
Four Lanes Infant School, Basingstoke

The King's Castle

I saw soldiers marching smartly in the dangerous battlefield.
I heard bats screeching loudly in the slimy dungeon.
I touched the mossy walls near the sticky dungeon.
I tasted the king's hot chocolate slowly in the clean kitchen.
I smelled chicken baking slowly in the black oven in the clean kitchen.

Elizabeth Cowley (6)
Four Lanes Infant School, Basingstoke

Untitled

I heard the funny king snoring loudly in the posh bedroom.
I spotted a beautiful princess dancing prettily in the pink ballroom.
I felt some armour hanging smartly in the armoury.
I tasted the strict king's hot chocolate bubbling quickly in the colourful dining room.
I sniffed thick smoke spreading quietly in the cool drawing room.

Blandine Thiebauld (6)
Four Lanes Infant School, Basingstoke

In The Castle

I smelled some roast chicken in the kitchen.
I heard noises in the dungeon.
I saw a shiny armour in the hallway.
I tasted slimy goo in the dungeon.
I touched a spiderweb in the dungeon.

Ty Minikin (6)
Four Lanes Infant School, Basingstoke

In The Castle

I saw golden armour standing in the long hallway.
I heard a corgi barking in the throne room.
I smelt a yummy banquet cooking in the hot oven.
I tasted a special potion in the potion room.
I stroked a blonde corgi in the king's royal room.

Joshua Vaughan (7)
Four Lanes Infant School, Basingstoke

In The Castle

I saw knights training slowly on the hilly battlefield.
I heard prisoners moaning quietly in the smelly dungeon.
I touched a sharp sword quickly in the armoury.
I tasted delicious chicken hungrily in the hot kitchen.
I smelled the king's smelly feet in his precious bedroom.

Ben Chambers (7)
Four Lanes Infant School, Basingstoke

In The Castle

I can hear a pretty princess singing loudly in the singing room.
I spotted one of the rich queen's nice corgis lying on a soft cushion.
I smelled some roast beef on the big table.
I tasted some red wine on the long, long table.
I touched some pretty flowers in the glass vase.

Faye Concannon (6)
Four Lanes Infant School, Basingstoke

In The Castle

I heard a red fire-breathing dragon in the deep dark forest.
I saw the royal king shouting across the long, long hall.
I stroked the fluffy corgi in the huge living room.
I tasted a delicious banquet in the special hallway.
I smelled roast chicken sizzling in the fragile pan.

Arun Tatter (6)
Four Lanes Infant School, Basingstoke

In The Castle

I can hear the strong wind blowing through the gates.
I can smell roast beef cooking in the hot oven.
I can taste roast beef in my mouth.
I can touch the queen's emerald crown.
I can see a beautiful horse in the stable.

Harry Randall
Four Lanes Infant School, Basingstoke

In The Castle

I heard scary ghosts howling across the crowded ballroom.
I spotted a fierce, brave knight fighting a red, horrible dragon.
I stroked a cute black and white cat on the amazing, golden throne.
I tasted a delicious, mouth-watering banquet at the feast table.
I sniffed smelly socks in the happy, friendly king's bedroom.

Yehia Alsaedi (6)
Four Lanes Infant School, Basingstoke

Untitled

I heard the swords clashing loudly on the massive battlefield.
I saw the queen's dresses hanging neatly in the dressing room.
I touched the sparkly crown carefully inside the crown room.
I tasted a delicious banquet hungrily in the grand dining room.
I smelled juicy chicken roasting in the hot oven.

Freddie Cox (6)
Four Lanes Infant School, Basingstoke

Untitled

I spotted the king's hot chocolate in the kitchen.
I heard the queen sleeping quietly in the big bedroom.
I touched tasty chicken in the scrumptious dining room.
I tasted the bread in the kitchen.
I smelled the king's corgis in the golden carriage.

Steven Webb (6)
Four Lanes Infant School, Basingstoke

In The Castle

I heard a burning oven in the dark scary kitchen.
I saw a delicious roast chicken with gravy in the secret room.
I touched a dusty, rusty window in the hallway.
I tasted a smelly worm cake with gravy on top.
I smelled the king's smelly socks in his bedroom.

Emmy Harfield (6)
Four Lanes Infant School, Basingstoke

In The Castle

I listened to knights training bravely in the scary battlefield.
I noticed armour hanging neatly in the armoury.
I felt the sparkly crown carefully in the beautiful throne room.
I munched on delicious roast chicken in the dining room.
I smelled the king's hot chocolate in the smelly and dirty kitchen.

Sam Goldsmith (7)
Four Lanes Infant School, Basingstoke

In The Castle

I heard scaly snapping crocodiles in the moat.
I spotted a red fire-breathing dragon, breathing out fire in his cave.
I felt a mossy drawbridge.
I tasted red wine, that makes your mouth water, in the kitchen.
I smelt the queen's perfume, it smelt like flowers, it was in her room.

Zach Roff (7)
Four Lanes Infant School, Basingstoke

In The Castle

In the castle . . . I saw a knight galloping quickly into the stone castle.
I heard rats scuttling quickly in the smelly dungeon.
I touched a silky dress hanging smartly in the queen's bedroom.
I tasted juicy fruit hungrily in the dining room.
I smelled smelly cows in the stony courtyard.

Harry Rolfe (6)
Four Lanes Infant School, Basingstoke

In The Castle

In the castle I heard a smelly giant stomping loudly in the dirty dungeon.
I saw a bright orange dragon blowing fire in the ballroom.
I touched a crown on the throne in the bedroom.

William Robins (6)
Four Lanes Infant School, Basingstoke

In The Castle

I heard a green spotty dragon breathing fire in the scary dungeon.
I saw a brown corgi playing in the bedroom.
I touched some cold armour standing in the dragon's lair.

Airon Martin (6)
Four Lanes Infant School, Basingstoke

In The Castle

I heard the king shouting with rage at a slave in his room.
I saw some shiny silver armour standing still in the hall.
I touched a soft cushion sitting still on a sofa in the lounge.

Henry Wheeler (6)
Four Lanes Infant School, Basingstoke

In The Castle

I heard a fire crackling in a hot fireplace.
I saw the servants cooking dinner in the old kitchen.

Dylan Mortimer (7)
Four Lanes Infant School, Basingstoke

The Astronaut's Journey

O ut of this world, on the moon,
U nder the blazing sun.
T he moon feels bouncy like blueberry jelly.
E ventually it's time to return to Earth,
R unning towards family with infinite stories.

S unny days missing space.
P ainting room for long-lost memories:
A mazing images of the solar system.
C all from space department . . .
E njoyment again!

Anna Silver (10)
Kent College Junior School, Canterbury

The Elephant And The Ant

The elephant's in my garden,
It's by my shed,
I have nowhere to get out,
The house is locked, the gates are rotten,
He is charging for me,
Like a big grey Ferrari,
And then gets destroyed by a tiny little ant,
Even though he is the giant!

He's coming closer
And now doesn't care about the old ant,
He's focusing on me,
With a big fat snout.

He's charging,
Faster and faster each time,
I just can't understand why.
He is still roaring like the grey Ferrari outside my back door,
He's getting closer,
He's turning around,
He whizzes past me as I hit the ground . . .

Lily Radford (10)
Kitebrook House, Moreton-In-Marsh

A Hairy Highland Cow

I once saw a hairy Highland cow
In a lush, green, grassy field
Gazing to her heart's content
Oh how she loved her meal.

Against the sunlit sky
Her colour was out of this world
She glowed in autumn rust and brown
Whilst stomping the leafy ground.

I loved her shaggy Highland mane
With all its tangles and knots
Which hung over her eyes
Although I think she could see quite a lot.

Her little calf jumped from behind a tree
Leaping and jumping, full of glee
The mummy, she watched her heifer with pride
Then she returned to eat her green grassy treasure.

I love the way she munches the grass
And swishes the flies away
How I wish I was a Highland cow
Eating and eating all day.

Sophia McAlpine (9)
Kitebrook House, Moreton-In-Marsh

Autumn

The orange leaves fall to the ground
And form a crunchy crisp carpet.
They fall to the ground like soft raindrops.

Shiny conkers glitter in the sun like glittering gems,
The colours of the leaves are like golden apples,
They twist in the dancing wind.

The pumpkin is as orange as a crackling fire
Flying higher and higher.

Max Craig (7)
Kitebrook House, Moreton-In-Marsh

Hedgehogs

Hedgehogs, hedgehogs with their wonderful spikes
Which everybody likes
Who crawl into the leaves in the evening.

Hedgehog, hedgehog, watch out spiky one
A fox is quite near
Though you feel no fear.

Hedgehogs, hedgehogs you all love flowers
There are worms in the earth underneath
So they stay in the flowers for hours and hours.

Hedgehog, hedgehog you need to be shy
So roll up into a ball with your spikes in a muddle
Because your running is slow and you might die
Roll up in a small brown huddle.

Hedgehogs, hedgehogs they're so sweet
We all of us should care
With their tiny pattering feet
But they're becoming so rare.

Loelia Bailey (9)
Kitebrook House, Moreton-In-Marsh

Chocolate Conkers

Chocolate conkers are beautiful brown,
with their lovely earthy colour.
They glint like chestnut stars in the sky.

Conker shells are like hedgehog skin.
They pop out of their shell
when they are ready to be found
by a young child on the ground.

Chocolate conkers cover the ground
like a blanket of chocolate.
They crackle and pop when people step on them
with their shiny winter boots.

Barnaby Coldridge
Kitebrook House, Moreton-In-Marsh

Chameleons

The chameleon with its many scales
Is almost the complete opposite of the whales -
And what a sight it would be
To see one in the sea.

Oh how camouflaged they are
But why don't they eat a chocolate bar?
They don't like you to peek
And they definitely don't reek.

They don't go to Mars
And they don't like being put behind bars.
Their boogly eyes can look mean
But their long curling tongues can be keen.

Just bear with them for they are cool
Even though they don't go in a pool.
Of all the animals they aren't the same
And no I am not playing a game -

Chameleons are weird!

Miller Sherwood (9)
Kitebrook House, Moreton-In-Marsh

The Elephant

One elephant, one elephant only
I think he was lonely.

This elephant walked very slowly
He looked rather holy.

This elephant moved like a lord
I think he was bored.

What might this elephant say
As he goes on his way?

'I'm one elephant, one elephant only
Very lonely, quite holy and bored!'

Lucy Tibbitts (10)
Kitebrook House, Moreton-In-Marsh

Komodo Dragon

They are savagely strong
But they smell like my aunty's welly
And they've got a belly
That wobbles like jelly.

They are rigid and scaly
And are fearless and mean
But are gorgeously green.

They don't have a beak
And they don't breathe fire
But they do eat meat.

They have long feet
And they have terrible claws
But you can hear hisses not roars.

I'd like to be one of them
And live in the sun
But in fact if I saw one - I'd run!

Jasper Brumpton (9)
Kitebrook House, Moreton-In-Marsh

The Elephant Of Art

This morning when I walked into school,
I saw him,
The big grey figure sitting in the corner of the art room.

His trunk was high towards the ceiling,
Brushing the lights,
Snuffling as he did this.

His shadow was huge,
It was like an eclipse that was there for only a few moments,
Because as it saw me,
It lumbered away,
Walking like a limping giant who'd lost a fight,
He had left a drawing on the roof of an . . .

Noah Kirkham (10)
Kitebrook House, Moreton-In-Marsh

Rats

Rats, rats, living in city sewers,
Never coming in homes,
Why, why aren't there fewer
Or even some living alone?

Desert rat, hot desert rat,
Scampering without disease,
Never getting chased by any cat,
Never suffering from fleas.

Rats, rats, never die out,
Always staying too near,
Why do you have such a small, thin snout
And cause us humans such fear?

Why, why don't we ever see you?
Why, why don't you ever come out?
Why do you hide in the shadows
Which only confirms our doubt?

Chloe Fermor (9)
Kitebrook House, Moreton-In-Marsh

Elephants All Day, All Night

They stamp along the sandy plain,
Where there is never rain,
They hunt around and have some fun,
Till the day is nearly done.

The starlit sky gives them light,
From the moon oh so bright.
Their trumpets give a shrill sound,
Which rumbles through the wispy ground.

Then at dawn they wake and stand,
Sending a warning across the land,
The elephants are hunting, it cries
But nothing ever has time to reply.

Sophie Marsden (10)
Kitebrook House, Moreton-In-Marsh

I Want To Be The First . . .

I want to be the first elephant to go to space,
A magical world,
A wonderful place,
It would be such fun to be the first one,
Up to Mars and beyond the stars,
Up to Saturn with its wonderful pattern,
I want to be the first elephant to go to space,
Maybe I'd meet space elephants along the way,
I would like to chat to them and hear what they say,
I'd trumpet a tune as I flew past the moon
And head my way for planet Neptune,
I want to be the first elephant to go to space,
Bright colours flashing by, crimson, scarlet, turquoise and jade,
As the mellow colours start to simmer down, to sleep,
For a night of memories I shall always keep.

Imogen Shackleton (10)
Kitebrook House, Moreton-In-Marsh

Guess What It Is!

They plod,
As loud as an army of marching giants.
Their trumpet is as triumphant as a gift from God;
The humongous ears they own waft like a geisha's fan.

The colour of them is muddy and sooty,
If you'd ask me I'd say they look like mountains.

They are as enormous as them too,
They are inspirational,
Also they're the most amazing view.

They've got their own act,
In the circus,
They're highly trained performers,
So now guess what it is, I bet you won't.

Ophelia Clarke (10)
Kitebrook House, Moreton-In-Marsh

Athena

Athena, Athena
Liked to drink Ribena.
She lived in the Greek kingdom
As the goddess of wisdom.
Did you know that Athena
Was also called Tritogenia?
Was Minerva when in Rome
But that was never home.
Born outside of Olympus
And maybe the daughter of Triton.
She was a woman of many aims
Who had so many names.
Athena, Athena,
Maybe try Orangena.

Imogen Brumpton (11)
Kitebrook House, Moreton-In-Marsh

The Warrior

Elephants stomp their big clumsy feet
On the ground like big Asian drums.
Elephants' tusks are as thick as rock
And their small eyes are like tennis balls.
Their tail slashing like a whip hitting flies
Down like World War II planes falling
And hitting the dusty floor.
They use their trunk like a shower
To cool them off.
Their big ears are as big as the moon.
I so wish I was an elephant and a warrior.
Don't you too?

Henry Austin (10)
Kitebrook House, Moreton-In-Marsh

Falling Leaves

Autumn leaves fall softly down,
Swirling, twirling to the ground
To make a carpet out of leaves.

Shiny conkers whoosh from the trees
Popping and crunching in the breeze,
They pop out of their shells with a prickly pop.

Squirrels scurry up the trees
To find nuts.
From the tree feathers fall
And blow in the wind.

William Cecil (7)
Kitebrook House, Moreton-In-Marsh

Autumn Colours

Autumn colours of burgundy red,
Crackling orange and chestnut brown.
Conkers falling off chestnut trees.

Autumn colours of golden yellow
And ruby-red leaves falling fast to the ground,
Bright red apples juicy and sweet.

Autumn colours of burning orange
And carpets like a rainbow.
Conkers falling down, down till they crack.

Theo Peake (7)
Kitebrook House, Moreton-In-Marsh

Gracefully

Gracefully the kingfisher flew
Gracefully the wind blew
Gracefully the dancer pirouetted
Gracefully the fox fled.

Gracefully the sea bobbed
Gracefully the stars twinkled
Graceful as the moonlight flickers
But the most graceful of all
Is the sleeping girl that lies beneath the stall.

Cecilia Loudon (8)
Kitebrook House, Moreton-In-Marsh

Stupidly

Stupidly the boy ran into the wall
Stupidly the dog tripped over the ball
Stupidly the astronaut launched the rocket
Stupidly the man opened the secret locket.

Stupidly the giant grows really tall
Stupidly the cat calls
Stupid is the clown - but stupidest of all
The games when we laugh, giggle and call.

Bob Rawlinson (8)
Kitebrook House, Moreton-In-Marsh

Swiftly

Swiftly the waves flow onto the beach.
Swiftly the child grabs the peach.
Swiftly the eagle hovers over the sky.
Swiftly the boy runs to say bye.

Swiftly the girl runs to the zoo.
Swiftly the astronaut bounces on the moon.
Swift is the cheetah, but swiftest of all
The boys giggle as they play football.

Oliver Riley (8)
Kitebrook House, Moreton-In-Marsh

Elegantly

Elegantly the ballerina twirled across the dance floor.
Elegantly the queen swept through the door.
Elegantly the bird flew down to the tree.
Elegantly the princess swirled as though she was free.

Elegantly the horse trotted down the road.
Elegantly the princess kissed the ugly toad.
Elegant is the golden eagle but most elegant of all
Is my mum getting ready for the ball.

Tabitha Moore (9)
Kitebrook House, Moreton-In-Marsh

Autumn Days

Raining leaves from the trees
That make a carpet out of leaves.

Swirling, twirling to the ground
Like ballerinas spinning softly.

Pumpkins are as bright as orange sunlight
And the stalk is like a green apple.

Mason Chambers (7)
Kitebrook House, Moreton-In-Marsh

Gracefully

Gracefully the ballerina twirled,
Gracefully in the rain the leaves curled.
Gracefully the bird flapped her wings,
Gracefully the river falls down in a fling.

Gracefully the princess swept through the door,
Gracefully the peacock went into the roar.
Graceful is the queen - but the most graceful of all
Is when my mum gets ready for the ball.

Charlotte Mackinnon (8)
Kitebrook House, Moreton-In-Marsh

Beautiful Autumn

Blowing leaves off the trees,
Dancing fairies in the wind,
Squirrels are collecting leaves
And nuts on the ground.

The conkers and the leaves
Are like a sparkling rainbow in the sky.
Colours of red and orange,
Yellow and brown.

Paige-Allen Thomas (7)
Kitebrook House, Moreton-In-Marsh

Autumn

Swirling, twirling autumn leaves
Snapping, cracking went the trees.

Rolling, rolling went the shiny brown conkers,
They look like glass marbles.

Scurry, scurry went the grey, fluffy squirrels,
They are busy finding juicy acorns!

William Noble (7)
Kitebrook House, Moreton-In-Marsh

My Monster

It has skin as crumbled as a paper.
My monster has teeth as yellow as the sun.
It has eyes as green as a dark pond.
My monster is as smelly as a rotten egg.
My monster's hair is as hairy as a hair ball.

Deven Trotman (7)
Kitebrook House, Moreton-In-Marsh

Sneakily

Sneakily the child put back the clock
Sneakily the dog stole my smelly sock
Sneakily my brother slammed the door
Sneakily the mouse scuttled over the floor.

Sneakily the child stole from the cookie jar
Sneakily a robber took the big red car
Sneaky is a criminal but the sneakiest of all
My little brother's grin when the vase falls.

Tabitha Little (8)
Kitebrook House, Moreton-In-Marsh

Energetically

Energetically the boy ran the 100 metres.
Energetically the dad played the beaters.
Energetically the dog sprinted to get the ball.
Energetically the man whizzed down the hall.

Energetically the girl brushed her hair.
Energetically the baby grabbed his bear.
Energetic is my brother but most energetic of all
The team running out to play football.

Mark Jonsson
Kitebrook House, Moreton-In-Marsh

Silently

Silently the leaves fell from the tree
Silently the driftwood floated in the sea
Silently the owl flew through the sky
Silently the bird learned how to fly.

Silently the lion crept up on its prey
Silently the night turned into day
Silent are the butterfly's wings but most silent of all is
The miaowing heard from the kitten's call.

Alice Hannah (8)
Kitebrook House, Moreton-In-Marsh

From Silence To Thunder

The stars shone bright
As the moon lit a light
What a wondrous sight to see
On a dark misty night
The elephants thunder
Through the shivering ground
Disturbing the silence
All around.

Scrase Duffy (10)
Kitebrook House, Moreton-In-Marsh

My Monster

My monster has eyes as green as disgusting buckets of slime.
It has feet as webbed as frogs' legs.
It has a roar like my dad snoring.
It smells like mouldy bananas.
It has teeth as sharp as knives.

Emily Szor (8)
Kitebrook House, Moreton-In-Marsh

The Seasons

One is warm.
One is cold.
One is of rebirth.
One's leaves fall, so I've been told.

The one that's warm.
Owns the sun.
Water fights erupt.
The air belongs to fun.

The one that's cold.
Owns the snow.
Snowmen are born.
And presents grow.

The one of rebirth.
Owns new life.
Of flowers and foals.
The values of husband and wife.

The one that leaves fall.
And the trees grow bare.
The warmth drops.
But I don't care!

The seasons of nature.
Each one unique.
Each individual.
Enrichment they seek.

Issy Colwell (11)
Leweston Junior School, Sherborne

Caeci Estis, Ut Cruciatus

Fire crackled, grenades boomed,
Bombs exploded in the darkened night,
A frosty shadow, cold as snow,
Swept over our heads like an icy wind.
Through the chaos, a crash was heard;
I saw the thick green gas creeping across no-man's-land.
The brave marched on, as the sea of poisonous green engulfed them.
Pointless screams and fires of guns, it was too late;
I breathed my last breath through gas-filled air . . .
It was over.

Eve Fidler
Leweston Junior School, Sherborne

Doleo Equidem Est In Bello

The open door of death was near,
Bombs dropped over me,
Men scream in the trenches - little light,
The canary drops quickly.
Gas! Gas! We dive in to the trench,
Running in fear as fast as our legs
Could carry us.
War is not to die for
But I wish I was already dead.
Yet the truth is . . .

Annabel Bruller (10)
Leweston Junior School, Sherborne

Senses

Out of this world
I can feel my heart beating because I am floating
Gently breathing at the same time.
I can see shining stars in the sky
The smell of moon dust is in the air
I can taste smoke from the sun
I can hear nothingness in the dark.

Kiara Holley-Paliano (6)
St John's CE School, Salisbury

Senses

Out of this world it smells good, hot and warm
Next I see aliens floating around me
I hear the twinkling stars touching each other
It tastes of moon dust
The soothing air touches my hand
It is amazing when it goes up my sleeves.

Oliver Bowden
St John's CE School, Salisbury

Senses

Space smells like sweet stars glittering through my nose
When I am in space I feel amazing and smooth
In space I taste hot gas soothing around me
In space I see some fantastic flashes going on
While I am in space I hear nothingness floating around me.

Nicole Roberts (6)
St John's CE School, Salisbury

Senses

Shining stars shine so brightly
I can taste air and moon dust
I can smell the burning fire from the sun
Out of this world feels like smooth air
I can hear nothingness.

Ruby Dicker
St John's CE School, Salisbury

Senses

Out of this world looks like shooting stars
Out of this world sounds like moon rocks
Out of this world feels like air
Out of this world tastes like berries
Out of this world smells like moon dust.

Daisy Baker
St John's CE School, Salisbury

Senses

Out of this world looks like dark shooting stars
Out of this world sounds like shooting stars
Out of this world feels wobbly
Out of this world tastes like air
Out of this world smells like moonlight.

Reo Ridout (5)
St John's CE School, Salisbury

Senses

Out of this world I can see shooting stars in the night sky
I am floating everywhere
I can taste moon dust
I can smell moon rocks
I can hear moon rocks crashing.

Chloe Hall
St John's CE School, Salisbury

Senses

Out of this world I see rocks floating in the sky
Out of this world I feel air swishing on my hand
Out of this world I smell a chocolate smell
Out of this world I taste sweet air on my tongue
Out of this world I hear nothingness.

Felix King
St John's CE School, Salisbury

Black Lightning On A Sunny Day

Dark-lighter
Human-frightener
Black-appearer
Sun-cheerer
Dark-flasher
Noise-crasher
Sun-stormer
Thin-former
Heart-stopper
Tree-chopper
Horror-maker
Ground-shaker
Big-shocker
Mind-locker.

Rubyleigh Emery (10)
St Peter's CE School, Aylesford

My Space Poem

Space adventures are so much fun
That's why we are going,
Hurry up, the countdown's begun,
The fire is already blowing.

5, 4, 3, 2, 1,
We are going to be there soon,
Are we going to the sun?
No, we are going to the moon!

Twirling round and round,
This is so much fun,
I can't see the ground,
Look, there's the sun.

We won't get there I bet,
We aren't there yet!

Hannah Burton (10)
St Peter's CE School, Aylesford

The Funny Hedgehog

Messy-eater
Worm-slurper
Slow-walker
Clever-sniffer
Day-sleeper
Leaf-spiker
Winter-hibernator
Night-walker
Sightseer
Super-swimmer
Thirsty-drinker
Tummy-warmer
A cute hedgehog.

Hannah Sparks (7)
St Peter's CE School, Aylesford

Hedgehog

Night-hunter
Day-sleeper
Leaf-spiker
Night-waker
Worm-slurper
Winter-hibernater
Food-finder
Cute-pricker
Breaker-leafer
Good-seeker
Food-storer
Good-hider.

Isla Trotter (7)
St Peter's CE School, Aylesford

Huggable Hedgehog

Worm-slurper
Star-gazer
Slow-walker
Clever-sniffer
Spiky-mover
Messy-eater
Day-sleeper
Night-hunter
Leaf-spiker
Winter-hibernator
Night-waker.

Gabi Goemans (7)
St Peter's CE School, Aylesford

The Hedgehog Poem

Day-sleeper
Worm-slurper
Night-hunter
Winter-hibernater
Leaf-cruncher
Night-eater
Less-spiky
Brown-spikes
Leaf-catcher
A super-spiker
A spiky-hedgehog.

Sophie Matthews (7)
St Peter's CE School, Aylesford

Tree Faller

People-stinger
Green-protector
Growing-er
Spiky-outer
Grisly-spikers
Spiky-conkers
Tree-faller
Green-cracker
Half-cracker.

Aiden Clark (8)
St Peter's CE School, Aylesford

The Wild Hedgehog

Day-sleeper
Night-awaker
Hibernater
Worm-slurper
Slug-eater
Brown-tumbler
Winter's-keeper
Food-storer
Cool-hider.

Emily Champion (7)
St Peter's CE School, Aylesford

Conkers Bonkers

Great-hitters
Spiky-fallers
Rough-feelers
Green-lookers
Smooth-growers
Even-strokers
Flat-touchers
Brown-ouchers.

Amber Gower (8)
St Peter's CE School, Aylesford

Winter

Winter feels like you want to snuggle up in your bed.
Winter smells like lovely, hot chocolate in a cup that is very, very hot.
Winter tastes like really good marshmallows in hot chocolate.
Winter looks like white snow on the ground.
Winter sounds like Christmas bells on a house.

Brooke Gillingham (7)
St Peter's CE School, Aylesford

Alien Hot Dogs

H appy alien hot dogs always eat cake.
O ver the lake making sure they don't step on the rake.
T aking a Flake.

D aring to eat a snack with a pancake.
O lives making mistakes, always breaking a snowflake.
G oing out of this world, you will always meet a whole load of aliens
hot dogs and a lot of snakes.

Lily Viner (9)
St Peter's CE School, Aylesford

Winter

Winter looks like a hot bonfire.
Winter tastes like toasted marshmallows.
Winter feels like making a snowman.
Winter smells like cookies burning.
Winter sounds like snowflakes hitting your window.

Jack Neal (6)
St Peter's CE School, Aylesford

Day And Night

Day-sleeper
Warm-maker
Worm-slurper
Cool-carder
Lazy-leaper.

Jodie Leigh Leigh Harris (7)
St Peter's CE School, Aylesford

The Night Of Halloween

It was the night of Halloween,
There was a full moon
A scream rang out on the Island of Doom!
Suddenly all kinds of spooky creatures came with their scary features.
There was a goblin and ghost, werewolf and witch,
Zombies that climbed out of a ditch.
They surrounded the castle that was Count Dracula's house,
But the only one in was a tiny mouse.
They went to his kitchen to cook up a brew of bat wings, eyeballs and pumpkin stew.
The party was ready to go
But what the monsters didn't know
That I was waiting in the loo to scare them with a great big, 'Boo!'

Jalani Odle (6)
Telscombe Cliffs Primary School, Peacehaven

My Garden

My garden looks nice
especially in sunrise.
It has many lovely flowers,
that look happy when it showers.
It has lots of bushes
with buzzy bees.

One day I found a bird singing a sweet lullaby.
I wanted to say hi!
but the bird was so shy,
and flew away up in the sky.

Yzabella Liezl Demaisip (6)
Telscombe Cliffs Primary School, Peacehaven

Cats Poem

Cats, cats, cats,
They always sit on their owners' laps.
Some are fat and some are small
But some are big and some are tall.
All day long they have loads of fun
Eat snacks and that's how some weigh a tonne!
They lounge in the sun but are usually always on the run
For hunting birds and chasing mice.
Cats, cats, cats, they're most of these things
But most of all they're very cool!

Monty Capildeo (6)
Telscombe Cliffs Primary School, Peacehaven

Starlord

His cape is sparkly gold,
He is fast and strong and bold.
Has thick, blonde hair,
That looks like a scruffy bear.
He can lift two cars with one hand!
He is the strongest hero in the land.
He can fly as quick as a flash,
To save people he will dash.
If you need him give him a call,
Starlord is the best of them all!

Stanley Webb (7)
Telscombe Cliffs Primary School, Peacehaven

My Guinea Pig

G reat
U nique
I ncredible like superheroes
N ose twitching
E xcellent
A mazing

P ets
I love
G uinea pigs!

Isla Young (6)
Telscombe Cliffs Primary School, Peacehaven

London

I went to London with my mum
I wanted my nan and grandad to come
On the way to the dungeon I saw a policeman with a truncheon.
I went on a boat ride.
I got a bit wet but I didn't mind I'm not dry yet.
We went to see Willy at the chocolate factory.
Nanny and Grandad and Mummy and me.

Sienna Price (6)
Telscombe Cliffs Primary School, Peacehaven

Firemen

Firemen are very brave,
In fires they have many people to save,
When the fire bell does ring,
Down the pole they will swing,
To race and put out the fire!

Jake Baldey
Telscombe Cliffs Primary School, Peacehaven

Help At Sea (RNLI)

R uling the waves that's what we do, saving lives like you and you.
N ow you know when you're in the sea, give us a wave there we will be.
L ifeboats, lifeboats on the sea, with a paramedic that will save me.
I love lifeboats on the sea, they save lives, that's the key.

Lucy Renshaw (7)
Telscombe Cliffs Primary School, Peacehaven

My Halloween Face Paint

My Halloween face paint is scary
And as I put the base on me
I looked in the mirror
I stared too hard
It splattered all over my face.

Kaitlin Cork (6)
Telscombe Cliffs Primary School, Peacehaven

Scary Halloween

'Great to meet you,' said the vampire to the ghost.
Don't press the button.
The zombie will jump out!
But this is just a fairground ride
There's no reason to run and hide.

James Barrow (6)
Telscombe Cliffs Primary School, Peacehaven

The Nearest Star

The nearest star is very, very far,
We could never, never reach it not even in a car.
I'd like to try but why, oh why?
Cos the nearest star is very, very far!

Max Hughes (6)
Telscombe Cliffs Primary School, Peacehaven

A Fish For A Dish

This is my fish
He is fit for a dish
And he tastes delish, delish, delish.

Phoenix Rogers (6)
Telscombe Cliffs Primary School, Peacehaven

Solar System

Eye-catcher
Dark-dark
Planets-emblaze
Spectacular-satellite
Echoing-echoes
Shining-stars
Stunning-view
Planets-orbiting
Comet-whizz
Alien-attackers
Roaring-rockets
Angry-astronauts
Like bears
Feel non-gravity
See infinite space.

Space, space, space.

Harrison Bradbury (8)
The James Oglethorpe Primary School, Upminster

Out Of This World

O utside
U niverse
T urquoise

O bject
F ast

T iny
H uge
I ndigo
S erious

W hite
O ctagon
R ound
L oud
D angerous.

Enrike Kukulskis (8)
The James Oglethorpe Primary School, Upminster

Out Of This World

O utstanding
U niverse
T urquoise

O ctagon
F oggy

T errific
H ole
I nteresting
S pooky

W orld
O ld
R ound
L oud
D rippy.

Madison Golding (7)
The James Oglethorpe Primary School, Upminster

Out Of This World

O utstanding
U niverse
T errifying

O ctagon
F erocious

T urquoise
H orrifying
I ndestructible
S cary

W arming
O range
R aging
L oud
D eafening.

Oscar Corbett (7)
The James Oglethorpe Primary School, Upminster

Out Of This World

O utstanding
U niverse
T errific

O versized
F uture

T ropical
H appy
I sland
S illy

W orld
O cean
R ealistic
L ife
D elightful.

Kyle Hewson (9)
The James Oglethorpe Primary School, Upminster

Out Of This World

O utside
U niverse
T ripping

O utstanding
F rightening

T asty
H igh
I ncredible
S lippery

W illing
O xygen
R ectangle
L ickable
D eep.

Tilly Ott (8)
The James Oglethorpe Primary School, Upminster

Out Of This World

O utstanding
U niversity
T asty

O ctagon
F un

T errified
H orrifying
I ncredible
S issy

W ow
O cean
R ealistic
L azy
D eath.

Niamh Shelley (8)
The James Oglethorpe Primary School, Upminster

Out Of This World

O ut of the box
U niverse
T errifying

O utstanding
F unny

T rembling
H orrible
I nspiring
S uperb

W onderful
O range
R inging
L ong
D elicate.

Grace Tyler (8)
The James Oglethorpe Primary School, Upminster

Out Of This World

O xygen
U niverse
T errible

O paque
F rightening

T urquoise
H orrible
I magine
S uperb

W ordless
O cean
R eal
L azy
D eath.

Jack Sanderson (7)
The James Oglethorpe Primary School, Upminster

Out Of This World

P lanets all over the universe that have amazing views and planets
rocky but dark.
L et us see amazing things up here so come and see.
A s different planets, 1, 2, 3, lots more too, rocky, bubbly, funny
and stripes, come and see more silly things.
N ets, fishing rods, dolls too and other things. I want them all,
there's pretty good stuff up here.
E ating up here is quite hard but we still cope with it, we have to eat
in our astro rocket.
T urning and twisting planets as the stars shine brightly.
S olar systems all around in space, Mars is making me feel hungry,
'I want food!'

Neve Willcocks (8)
The James Oglethorpe Primary School, Upminster

Solar System

S olar system
O utstanding
L oud
A pocalyptic
R are black holes

S pace shuttle
Y oung sun
S un
T ime
E xplosions
M ounds.

Ben Stokes (8)
The James Oglethorpe Primary School, Upminster

My Space Poem

S pace is a wonderful place.
O utstanding! People love the moon because it is outstanding.
L ight! The moon is beautiful because of its light.
A mazing! Do you think the moon is amazing?
R epeating planets phase the sun.

S ee space, it's brain-bursting.
Y es, space is lovely.
S pacemen visit the moon.
T elescopes are very good for seeing space.
E xciting space, it's exciting because it's beautiful.
M y sisters and me see space with a telescope.

Olivia Thomas (8)
The James Oglethorpe Primary School, Upminster

Out Of This World

S pace is a wonderful place to explore
O ver the world you can see countries and water
L and and sea are different colours
A gainst the Earth like a smoking fireball is Mars
R emember Neil Armstrong, who was the first on the moon

S ave your strength for it is a long way away
Y et space won't end, for it continues forever
S ystems that continue
T urn around does the Earth
E ver it will last, it never ends
M y world, your world, it never ends.

Anjolaoluwa Adeniji (7)
The James Oglethorpe Primary School, Upminster

Space

Outstanding-planets
Purple-planets
Lovely-sight
Sensational-place
Dark-place
Breathtaking-place
Amazing-area
Infinity-sights
Alien-life
Whizzing-rockets
And that's space, space, space!

Jacob Cornwell (8)
The James Oglethorpe Primary School, Upminster

Spaceship

S tars glistening in your eyes,
P lanets as big as the night sky,
A liens spinning around the world,
C omets going past very fast, making a dusty smell,
E choes echoing.
S pectacular view,
H ot, burning sun, so is Mars,
I nfinite sky,
P umping heart in the dreaded silence.

Isobel Davies (8)
The James Oglethorpe Primary School, Upminster

Spaceship

S tunning view,
P lanets orbiting the sun,
A nd out-of-this-world stars,
C omets whizzing,
E xcellent echoes,
S atellites flying as fast as a cheetah,
H ear the hot sun sizzle,
I nfinite actually,
P ractically cool!

Jessica Rogers (9)
The James Oglethorpe Primary School, Upminster

Out Of This World

P lanet Mars is very close to the sun
L ava is only at Mars or the sun
A planet it can be big or small
N othing is in space, it is empty
E verything happened on space
T alent work to get into space.

Christina SadikaJ (8)
The James Oglethorpe Primary School, Upminster

Out Of This World

S ome people who I know want to visit space.
P eople have visited the moon in space before.
A planet is called Mars.
C ool people visit space.
E arth has lots of water on it.

Louis Geater (7)
The James Oglethorpe Primary School, Upminster

Out Of This World

S ome people want to visit space because it has a space buggy.
P eople have visited the moon in space before.
A planet is called Mars.
C ool people visited space.
E arth is part of the moon.

Millicent Murray (8)
The James Oglethorpe Primary School, Upminster

Out Of This World

S pace is an amazing place.
P lanets are brilliant.
A stronauts are funny.
C ome and see the amazing space!
E normous planets in space.

Archie Powell (7)
The James Oglethorpe Primary School, Upminster

Out Of This World

S pace is an amazing place.
P lanets are beautiful and big.
A ir, there's no oxygen in space.
C an you see in the dark?
E normous planet in space.

Ruby Elsdon (8)
The James Oglethorpe Primary School, Upminster

Out Of This World

S uper cool space.
P lanet rock.
A wesome satellite.
C ool stars.
E xcellent solar system.

Dylan Teece (7)
The James Oglethorpe Primary School, Upminster

Out Of This World

S pectacular place, come and look.
P lenty of planets you will see.
A stronauts floating around and around.
C an you see planets? 1, 2, 3, everywhere, come and see.
E xcellent place so come and visit one day.

Chloe Taylor (8)
The James Oglethorpe Primary School, Upminster

Out Of This World

S pace is an amazing place to be
P lanets are excellent
A mazing view when you are on the moon
C ome and see the planets
E normous planets in space.

Georgia Phillipson (8)
The James Oglethorpe Primary School, Upminster

Out Of This World

S pace is a dangerous place.
P lanets are exciting.
A stronauts live in a rocket.
C ome on the moon.
E xplore the planets.

Brandon Phillips (9)
The James Oglethorpe Primary School, Upminster

Out Of This World

S ee the planets in space.
P lanets like Mars in space.
A nd there are lots of other places, like Pluto.
C ome and see what it's like on other planets.
E at your stuff upside down.

Jude Butler (9)
The James Oglethorpe Primary School, Upminster

Out Of This World

Dark, mysterious,
Breathtaking, gloomy, lifeless,
Cold, dull, colossal.

Mia Sweeney (9)
The James Oglethorpe Primary School, Upminster

Out Of This World

Cold, mysterious
Dull, sinking, dark, bright, big, grey
Cold, fantastic, dark.

Joshua Hobbs (8)
The James Oglethorpe Primary School, Upminster

Out Of This World

Abandoned, lifeless
Freezing, cold, horrifying
Dark, mysterious.

Glen Wiggins (8)
The James Oglethorpe Primary School, Upminster

Out Of This World

Cold, disaster, dark
Mysterious, dull, deadly
Gloomy, spooky, cold.

George Seaman (9)
The James Oglethorpe Primary School, Upminster

Out Of This World - Haiku

An amazing place,
Smells of mint choc chip ice cream,
I feel wonderful!

Kyla Dixson (8)
The James Oglethorpe Primary School, Upminster

Out Of This World

Cold, incredible
Dark, dull and mysterious
Breathtaking, lifeless.

Noah Smith (7)
The James Oglethorpe Primary School, Upminster

Out Of This World

Gloomy, spooky, dark
Mysterious, deadly, dull
Disaster, cold, ends.

Katie Waller (8)
The James Oglethorpe Primary School, Upminster

Out Of This World

Cold, scary, lifeless
Dull, dark, end, mysterious
Incredible, wrecked.

Zoë Roberts (7)
The James Oglethorpe Primary School, Upminster

Out Of This World!

Smell of lavender.
All around the misty sky.
In a big, weird world!

Rebecca Francs (8)
The James Oglethorpe Primary School, Upminster

Out Of This World!

Scary like a ghost.
As misty as a summer.
You cannot breathe there.

Jayma Thomas (8)
The James Oglethorpe Primary School, Upminster

Out Of This World

Abandoned, lifeless
Freezing, cold, mysterious
Dark, horrifying.

William Jones (8)
The James Oglethorpe Primary School, Upminster

Out Of This World

Incredible, dull
Dark, mysterious, freezing
Cold, sinking, planet.

Tillie Callis (7)
The James Oglethorpe Primary School, Upminster

Out Of This World

Lifeless, timeless, end.
Abandoned, destroyed, dark, dull.
Colossal, cold, start.

Tyler Robertson (9)
The James Oglethorpe Primary School, Upminster

Out Of This World

Misty, lifeless, cold,
Dull, mysterious, foggy,
Colossal, wrecked, end.

Lexie Ive & Jada Nnodim (8)
The James Oglethorpe Primary School, Upminster

Out Of This World

Timeless, round, haunted,
Gigantic, lonely, gloomy,
Battered, broken, ball.

Emma Chambers (8)
The James Oglethorpe Primary School, Upminster

Fizz, Bang, Pop

Fizz, bang, pop
as the fireworks explode
into the night sky.
screams from the children
chanting, 'We want more.'
The darkness suddenly gets
interrupted by the bright
colours shooting like
shooting stars in the sky.
Babies are frightened.
Kids are hypnotised.
Adults are fascinated.
Finally the fireworks
stop but . . .
Remember, remember the
5th of November.

Amy Parkin (11)
Westbury On Trym CE Academy, Bristol

The Display

I feel the night air stroking my face with his cold hands,
My hand building up with sweat; becoming clammy.
The sweat is trickling down my forehead;
the silence building up in suspense.

Then suddenly . . . bang! I hear the sky lighting up
with beams of sparkly light.
Boom, fizz, crackle, blast,
the sound flooding into my ears.

I look up to the sky and see purple, green, gold
and red, illuminating the night sky.
The sparks painting the black canvas.
They pirouette endlessly like ballerinas,
spinning until out of sight.

I breathe in through my nose
and fire and burning embers fill my nose.
But the mild, cool air refreshes my face.

And the display is finished.

Florence Spear (10)
Westbury On Trym CE Academy, Bristol

A Sparkly Night

Fireworks exploding with colours so bright,
Lighting up the starless, shiny night,
Catherine and her beautiful sparks,
Glistening in the gloomy darks,
Red, yellow
Orange and green,
What a fabulous, remarkable sight to be seen,
Look at the crowd, they're all smiling,
And the fireworks are truly flying.

Now it's time to pack up and go,
For it is the end of our amazing, fantastic firework show!

Olivia King (10)
Westbury On Trym CE Academy, Bristol

Firework Fantasy

Fast-flier
Sky-shooter
Extreme-exploder
Loud-screamer
Blasting-boomer
Colour-maker
Endless-enjoyer
Happiness-preventer
Fast-fader
Ash-dropper
Ember-turner
Fire-leaver
Memory-leaver
Slow-dier
Quick-returner.

Lily Randhawa (10)
Westbury On Trym CE Academy, Bristol

The Nights Of Fire

Remember, remember when screaming ones lit up the sky,
Up to the sky, they spin a journey to the stars,
Once they turned into stars and fell upon us,
like rain in regal colours.

Up they go, the whizzing flame fire-makers come,
Crashing down, sending sound into our ears,
Crash, bang, scream!
Night as black as soot, motionless people,
Stand stock-still watching the beauty.

They whisper some of them as they go up,
Fireworks are fire, they are stars,
They are as colourful as a field full of flowers,
But when they end, they plunge down and die.

Megan Saunders (11)
Westbury On Trym CE Academy, Bristol

Firework

F rightening balls of fire zoom into the distance as the rockets claim their territory
I ntense Catherine wheels spin round whilst the audience scream excitedly
R ockets. Noise. Colour. Darkness. Sparks fly into the sky where everyone cheers at the sight.
E ncouragement comes from the Catherine wheel. Shouts come from the rockets, cackles come from the sprinklers
W ork comes from the sparklers as they light up the night
O n the evening sky, the fireworks slowly tear the sky away
R ed glows light up the sky like there's no tomorrow
K ing of the brilliant, beautiful fireworks, the . . . camera stands tall.

David McGregor (10)
Westbury On Trym CE Academy, Bristol

Fireworks Bright

Fireworks bright,
Lighting up the night,
Rockets, Catherine wheels, all of them unique.
Red, yellow, blue, so many colours to choose,
And then suddenly, ***boom!***
They burst in the air,
Sharing their flare with the sky,
Then a few seconds later,
The ember dies out.
The fireworks have now left our presence,
And the only thing left is the shadow from the night sky.

Rabia Hassan (10)
Westbury On Trym CE Academy, Bristol

Fireworks

Remember, remember the 5th of November, people are shouting in the park.
Children hear the fireworks and burst into tears.
Everyone is happy talking and laughing, celebrating the Guy Fawkes day.
Boys are running in the cold and hold their hands and sing of happiness.
Catherine wheels spinning in the sky as the wind is blowing.
Fireworks exploding with lots of colours.
Celebrating the historic day of Guy Fawkes.

Oliver Vowles (10)
Westbury On Trym CE Academy, Bristol

Fireworks

High up in the night sky,
Lies a beautiful delight.
As pretty, colourful fireworks,
Scatter far and wide.

Blue, orange and purple,
Screaming as they hurtle.
Green, yellow and indigo,
Way up high they go.

So everyone sit back, all enjoy the show!

Ben Beggs (10)
Westbury On Trym CE Academy, Bristol

Owls

World-waker
Mouse-hunter
Good-flyer
Loud-whistler
Quick-darter
Fast-swooper
Warm-sneaker
Tree-sleeper
Fluffy-feather
Food-tricker
Person-annoyer
Insect-eater
Leaf-shaker
Day-sleeper
Night-stalker
Sneaky-hider
Prey-chaser

Just the best ... owls.

Azura Elizabeth Smith
Woodside Primary School, Ruardean Woodside

Halloween

H appiness at night
A t night I knock on the door and have sweets
L ights on when it is dark
L ooks scary in the dark
O pen creaky doors
W itches ride their brooms
E ats all sweets for trick or treat
E veryone enjoys themselves
N o one wants to go home.

Ella Kear (7)
Woodside Primary School, Ruardean Woodside

Amazing Wolves

Amazing-runner
Meat-eater
High-jumper
Strong-stealer
Loud-howler
Night-crawler
Nasty-creature
Fish-hunter
Water-drinker
Good-listener
Meat-finder
Scary-predator

Unlike any other wolf.

Jeremy Maxwell
Woodside Primary School, Ruardean Woodside

The Cute Bunny

High-jumper
Carrot-stealer
Fat-walker
Slow-wagger
Chubby-eater
Leg-leaper
Fluffy-helper
Stinky-breather
Vegetable-finder
Scary-predator
Sneaky-snatcher
Midnight-picker

Unlike any other bunny.

Jacob Wragg-Jones
Woodside Primary School, Ruardean Woodside

Puppies

Puppies are small
They like chasing a ball
Try to run as fast as a car
But not getting very far

Puppies like going on walks
Barking loud when he talks
In the garden digging holes
Trying hard to find some moles.

Demi Harbinson (7)
Woodside Primary School, Ruardean Woodside

My Dogs

Sparkling fur I like to pat
Running and chasing the neighbours' cat
Muddy walks in the woods
Fetch sticks like they should

Playing ball with each other
Just like me and my brother
Doing tricks for yummy treats
Being naughty ripping bed sheets.

Jayden Jones
Woodside Primary School, Ruardean Woodside

Kittens

K eeps playing with toy string
I nside keeps pushing plates off the table
T ummy soft and furry
T ummy cute and fluffy
E ars fluffy and small
N ose is small and cute
S mall tail that flaps.

Neo Gardiner
Woodside Primary School, Ruardean Woodside

Dracula

Only comes out at night,
Run and hide,
Always hides from daylight,
Can keep bats in his castle,
Upside down bats,
Loves to drink blood,
Always hides from the sun,
Dracula.

Bobby Potter-Thomas
Woodside Primary School, Ruardean Woodside

Space

S paceships in the sky,
P retty stars come out of the sky,
A liens shoot spacemen,
C ool spacemen are heroes,
E very day the moon comes up.

Thomas Hamm
Woodside Primary School, Ruardean Woodside

Aliens

On Mars they are alive
UFOs are what they drive
Guns to laser the human race
When they travel up to space.

Callum Alexander Johnston (7)
Woodside Primary School, Ruardean Woodside

Portugal - Haiku

Sunny and rainy
The sky is very pretty
It is colourful.

Kyran Peter Jack Meek (8)
Woodside Primary School, Ruardean Woodside

My Dear Mum

Sweet as sugar,
Beautiful as a peacock,
More adorable than anything,
You my dear mum.

Nice beautiful eyes,
Cheeks as rosy red,
Face as white as snow,
Beautiful as a flower bed.

My dear mum
I love you a lot,
You are very caring,
So I will never be hurt.

I will always obey you,
And never make you cry,
I will always be nice to you,
And never tell a lie.

You are the,
Best in the world,
I love you,
And you love me . . . a lot.

Thank you for everything,
You are very glamorous,
You can do some resting,
When I am big enough.

Samragyi Pokhrel (9)
Yeading Junior School, Hayes

World War One

Bombs fighting, ***boom!***
Innocent people dying,
Gunpowder floating in the air,
The sadness and death spreading.

Screaming and crying,
Blood drops dripping as tears down a cheek,
People feeling terrified, trying to survive,
Chanting for help.

Danger is lurking in each corner,
No one is trusted,
Fun is ended in a second,
Schools getting bombed.

People screaming before their death,
Friends and family never seen again,
Love being bombed down,
No one there, you're all alone . . .

Until you hear the bombs go, ***boom!***
And the trigger of the sniper, ***click,***
Zeppelins fly over you
Others are here to fight.

Children getting lost,
Love of family destroyed,
Starving, injured people,
Who will protect them?

Shivleen Gill (10)
Yeading Junior School, Hayes

The Warehouse

My heart thumped as I stepped on the cold, metal ground,
Several dead mice is what I found,
All I saw was metal and pipes,
Run like a coward, I might,
But I stayed in my position,
To venture on was my decision.

But then I heard something,
It was a loud shriek that came from nothing,
But then I saw the stretched shadow,
Looming across the metallic meadow,
I still didn't see the person that caused this,
But when I did, it looked like thick, black mist.

It was then I decided to run,
For this was not fun,
Being chased by an object with no appearance,
And it seemed to be finding me a nuisance,
When I was near to freedom I looked back,
And finally saw the thing was big, dark and black.

I saw his tail curl,
This thing was out of this world,
It grabbed me and shook me for fun,
He certainly took all air out of my lungs,
I was on my last breath,
And finally he stabbed me in the chest.

Zaim Abdin (10)
Yeading Junior School, Hayes

Homework, I Love You

Homework, I love you. I think that you're great.
It's wonderful when you keep me up late.
I think you're the best when I'm totally stressed,
Preparing and cramming all night for a test.

Homework, I love you, what more can I say?
I love to do hundreds of problems each day.
You boggle my mind and you make me go blind,
But still I'm ecstatic that you were assigned.

Homework, I love you, I tell you it's true,
There's nothing more fun or exciting to do,
You're never a chore, for it's you I adore,
I wish that our teacher would hand you out more.

Homework, I love you, you thrill me inside,
I'm thrilled with emotions, I'm fit to be tied,
I cannot complain when you frazzle my brain,
Of course, that's because I'm completely insane.

Homework, you're the best, you help me learn,
In maths with all the shapes you make me turn,
Homework, you're always by my side,
Making the school journey an exciting ride.

Tia Sanghani (10)
Yeading Junior School, Hayes

8 Things Found In Yeading's Playground

Shimmering raindrops, tipper tapper off a crying cloud.
Thud! Rocks falling as hard as bricks!
Crunch! Golden leaves come trembling down trees . . .
Squish! Squash! Tomatoes crying for their mummies.
Tiles as strong as ten elephants, a metro can't break it!
Swoosh! Feathers floating in the whistling wind,
Eee! Argh! Spiky, holey leaves as sharp as knives.
Footsteps as loud as a lion eating its prey.

Akshayian Ganesharatanam (9)
Yeading Junior School, Hayes

The Universe

The universe so bright and blue,
Creatures beyond the stars,
Nothing like you.

Aliens, cybermen, robots and more,
Travel the universe to see
What I saw!

Things out of this world,
Bursting with colours, wow!

Slimy, beastly, noble, evil and ugly,
More than disgusting,
More than a monkey, wow!

OMG! It seems so ugly,
I will never go there,
More than a donkey!

It's final! I'm not going there,
It seems so creepy, wow!
This is out of this world!
Oh! Wait, that's what we're talking about,
Out of this world!

Drishtee Sookraj (9)
Yeading Junior School, Hayes

Space

Space, space, why are you there?
Space, space, why don't you have hair?

Space, space, do you like chocolate bars,
If not why do you have Mars?

Space, space, are you there?
If so stop treating me like a bear.

Space, space, listen to me!
Else I'll change my name to Lee.

Mikaiel Shuaib (10)
Yeading Junior School, Hayes

Don't Tell 'Em

Didn't do my homework
Don't tell 'em
Didn't water the plants
Ain't bothered

Didn't feed the fish
Don't tell 'em
Didn't get the food
Jus' chillin'

Got a bad report
Don't tell 'em
Failed my test
Ain't worried

Failed my SATs
Don't tell 'em
Don't tell 'em
Please don't tell 'em
I'll tell 'em!

Balraj Singh Virdi (9)
Yeading Junior School, Hayes

Baby Brother

Dummy-sucker
Smelly-nappy
Racket-maker
Homework-destroyer
Wants-attention
Anything-eater
Milk-guzzler
Hardly sleeps
Big-annoyer
Peppa Pig-watcher
Unlike any other
My baby brother.

Jasmin Kaur Sidhu-Bansal
Yeading Junior School, Hayes

What Am I?

Quick-runner
Computer-genius
Strong-fighter
Clever-clogs
Mind-reader
Good-footballer
Fast-worker
House-cleaner
Messi-fan
Pencil-breaker
Quick-sharpener
Head teacher
Fashion-designer
Electric-conductor
Thunder-coward
Metal-liker.

I am a robot.

Ahees Thevarajah (9)
Yeading Junior School, Hayes

All About Me

Man Utd-supporter
Arsenal-hater
Pet-buyer
Cards-collector
Friend-maker
Water-drinker
Football-lover
Goal-scorer
Card-trader
Phone-watcher
God-believer
Promise-keeper
Tea-maker.

Vigash Tharamavarthan
Yeading Junior School, Hayes

Who Am I?

Fast-runner
Quick-turner
Long grass-lover
No-smiler
Food-searcher
Good-smeller
Meat-eater
Shop-hater
Alive-eater
Noisy-disliker
Light-hater
Night-hunter
Deer-chaser
Powerful-swimmer
Poacher-hater

What am I ? A tiger.

Shuceyb Moalim (9)
Yeading Junior School, Hayes

Out Of This World

My alien's name is Buto.
She lives on planet Pluto.
She really likes eating beans,
But she hates being mean.
She has lots of mates,
And she has lots of dates.
She likes writing,
But she also likes biting.
She plays in the snow,
And she likes biting her toes!
She has a very big head,
And she likes going to bed!
Oh my, oh my,
I have to say bye!

Nisha Saroye
Yeading Junior School, Hayes

Granny Is . . .

Granny is fired dumpin' an' run-dung
Coconut drops an grater cake
Fresh ground coffee in the morning
When we wake

Granny is loading up the donkey basket
Full on market day with fresh snapper
And she says to me 'Where is your Papa,'
And I say, 'I have no idea.'

'I can take you home and we can live alone,
Granny is making tea, hot tea,'
She says to me, 'I'm very nice, do you want some rice?'
And I say, 'No thank you I need to go to the loo.'

She says back, 'The toilet is on the left, upstairs,
On the right, straight, then left,
Then right, then straight, then it's there.'

Rayaan Ahmed (9)
Yeading Junior School, Hayes

Me In The Water

I took a dive in the water,
And I felt so much smaller,
I saw two massive whales,
As the boat on top of me sails,
I swam with a fish and the fish knew,
And behind him was his crew.

The great white shark whizzed past,
As no other fish came in its path,
The fishes swam behind,
As the shark knew in its mind,
Wow! I saw a big, grey machine,
And I watched it like I was watching a scene,
Long and green weeds were standing out and 'Argh!' I shout.

Gurshan Basra
Yeading Junior School, Hayes

My Brother

Cartoon-lover
Hair-puller
Bad-runner
Paint-lover
Football-crazy
Homework-snatcher
Anything-chewer
Phone-dialler
Loud-shouter
Mess-maker
Milk-drinker
Pencil-biter
Smelly-pooer
Night-crier
Unlike any other
My brother.

Harnimrat Sidhu
Yeading Junior School, Hayes

The Sun

Sun, sun you're so bright,
You're so bright as moonlight,
Sun, sun, you're a star,
You're brighter than a star,
Sun, sun, you give heat,
You give heat to everyone.
Sun, sun, you're so hot,
You're as hot as a volcano.
Sun, sun, you're so special,
You're so special with the brightness.
Sun, sun you're so far,
You're as far as a meteorite.
Sun, sun you're so good,
You're as good as chocolate.

Muteen Ali-Choudhrey (10)
Yeading Junior School, Hayes

What Do I Get In The Morning?

I wake up with a smile on my face,
Wondering what will happen today,
I'm burning with excitement,
What will happen?
But you know what,
I have a pancake on my plate,
Crispy and sweet goes in my mouth,
After I will chillax on my couch,
Then I'll transfer it in my pouch,
And go to the shop and buy another couch,
A trip to the zoo on a Sunday morning,
Look at the tigers, not so boring,
The turtles are just stomping and stomping,
Never be naughty with the duckies,
That was just quite a day,
Looking forward to another day!

Sukhmani Hayre (9)
Yeading Junior School, Hayes

12 Things Found In Yeading's Playground

Rolling round tomatoes squashed with juicy flesh,
Jet-black feathers fly across the world,
Crunch go the leaves by the stepping of boisterous kids,
Cold winds sigh at the deserted playground.

Sponge balls cry as their body falls away,
Warm wood chips are snapping,
Trees dance to a ponderous pattern,
Litter cries down to the ground.

Clouds hug whilst sobbing the rain,
Drooping plants wilt for water,
Berries hang on a prickly thorn,
Leaves shuffle as the wind breathes calmly . . .

Sopna Shanmugathas (9)
Yeading Junior School, Hayes

Who Am I?

Tea-maker
Story-teller
Nutella-hater
TV-watcher
Radio-listener
Football-lover
Shoe-shopper
Car-washer
Car-fixer
Toast-maker
Mum-lover
Mess-cleaner
Good-runner
Busy-baller
Unlike any child.

Roshan Kundi (9)
Yeading Junior School, Hayes

The Dipped Girl

Hi, my name is Michelle but everyone calls me the dipped girl.
I fall off my bike,
I fall down off the slippy mud and get soaked in the rain.
I fall in raspberry jam and come out pink.
I fall into the bath tub and come out soggy.
I fall off the pavement and fall onto the grass,
Oh no, I've got a stain on my trousers.
I slip on the tiles and end up on the wet floor.
I find myself in the washing machine and guess what? I get soaked.
I slip on the stairs, I fall onto the carpet and slide,
Guess what? I ended up in the smelly toilets.
I fall off the ladder and the black paint spills on me.
I was walking and the dog licked me.
So you see I get dipped in everything,
So do you know why they call me that now . . . ?

Vaishnavi Namanather (9)
Yeading Junior School, Hayes

Who Am I?

Big-burper
All time-wailer
Dummy-sucker
Short-sleeper
Nappy-wearer
Babbles
Trips over
Attention-seeker
Milk-drinker
Parent-stayer
Brother-annoyer.

Who am I?
A baby!

Neil Sorthia (9)
Yeading Junior School, Hayes

Monsters On The Moon

The monsters on the moon are funny
Old jokes, they don't know what they're doing half the time.
Every day they don't go to bed or even brush their yellow teeth,
Strange creatures what do the eat on the moon?
Why are their teeth so sunshine yellow?
Well let's find out the funny old moon creatures are messing all about,
When they're born, do they wear a bib and cry all night or feed on milk,
Because if they did their teeth would be white,
Oh these funny old moon creatures who would have known they also had purple, pongy spots.
Now you know who these silly old moon creatures are.

Heba Agal (7)
Yeading Junior School, Hayes

The Magic Box!

(Based On 'Magic Box' By Kit Wright)

I will put in my magic box,
The smirk of a lovely, white snowman,
The gleam of the full moon,
A final deafening roar of a fierce dinosaur.

In my box I will put,
The tip of a horn from a unicorn,
The golden heart of a butterfly,
Fluttering heartbeat of a fairy flying like an elegant, white dove.

In my magic box I will put,
The roaring fire dancing up and down,
My box is fashioned from gleaming ruby,
The hinges are made of horseshoes.

Sopisa Mohanachselvan (9)
Yeading Junior School, Hayes

5 Things Found In Yeading's Playground

Gleaming raindrops drip-dropping onto the malleable trees,
I don't even know what I see,

Tomatoes splitting their own eyes,
I don't even know their size! ***Squelch!***

Crunchy, crispy, laughing leaves,
Swaying across the glamorous breeze,

Fierce feathers already soft and gentle,
I don't even know how they settle?

The rigid bark is being kicked by obnoxious children,
And adults want peace and quiet . . .

Yaqub Hassan (9)
Yeading Junior School, Hayes

Aliens

Aliens are cute, they are amazing too . . .
They are small, they live on a big planet
I wonder why they are small?
They have lots of arms and legs,
They eat green, fresh leaves and grass,
They are scary.

They have three eyes,
They have black antennae,
They are scared because of us,
They are amazing,
They are in space,
They live on a planet.

Bhavika Athiparan (7)
Yeading Junior School, Hayes

The Mystery Object

Good-watcher
Still-stayer
Shape-mixer
Weather-watcher
Clear-looker
Mouth-opener
Easy-breaker
Invisible-feeler
Air-bringer
Silent-liver

What am I?
A window.

Fakeha Mirza (10)
Yeading Junior School, Hayes

What Am I?

Game-changer
Fast-runner
Serious-player
Good-controller
Epic step-overs
Healthy-eater
Ginormous-helper
Hard-kicker
Goal-mucker
Record-breaker.

Who am I?
Pele, the legend.

Nishanjit Tamber (9)
Yeading Junior School, Hayes

Guess Who I Am?

Embarrassing
Twist and turner
Shout and screamer
Grey hair grower
Loud snorer
Voice loser
Bad listener
Cartoon lover
Destroyer
Felt-tip pen waster

My little sister!

Aaliyah Cumberbatch (9)
Yeading Junior School, Hayes

Who Am I?

I fly
I glide
I soar
I'm white
I'm strong
I'm elegant
I'm graceful
I'm gorgeous
I swim
I'm helpful
I'm kind.

Mariam Abdilahi (9)
Yeading Junior School, Hayes

Who Am I?

Movie-watcher
Baking-lover
Monkey-hater
Gymnastics-liker
Friends-maker
Tea-drinker
Mummy-helper
Pencil-biter
Sister-annoyer
Packed lunch-loser
It's me, Riya.

Riya Valji
Yeading Junior School, Hayes

What Am I?

I'm a furry little creature
I'm a meat eater
I'm an enormous thing
I'm scary but cute
I'm a super smeller
Sometimes I'm naughty
I'm a quick muncher
I've got sharp claws
But I'm a fast runner
What am I?
I am a bear!

Sagana Baskar (9)
Yeading Junior School, Hayes

My Alien Called Kate

My alien is called Kate.
She lives on an unknown planet called Tate.
Kate has blue skin,
And she gets food from the bin.
You think she's really nice,
But if you touch her, you have to think twice.
She has big, round eyes,
And she hates telling lies.
Kate has colourful hair,
And her pet is a bear!
She is as beautiful as a princess!

Kiran Saroye (8)
Yeading Junior School, Hayes

Cats

Tree-climber
Tea-spiller
Never-lazy
Fish-eater
Cute-paws
Really-funny
So-pretty
Rat-killer
Sock-warmer
Sometimes friendly.

Hannan Ahmed (10)
Yeading Junior School, Hayes

Wally The Alien

Mind-reader
Stranger-looker
Colour-changer
Jelly-belly
Slimy-body
Human-hater
Space-lover
Cubed-face
Claw-holder
Human-transformer.

Asvin Srimurgan (9)
Yeading Junior School, Hayes

My Alien Gaspud

Grumpy ears, slimy tears,
Amazing sense of smell,
Slurpy lips and dirty tips,
This is about my Gaspud,
Picks his nose,
Unusual toes,
Dark coloured teeth,
Really loves all his meat,
This is about my Gaspud.

Yonathan Aklilu (7)
Yeading Junior School, Hayes

My Sweet World

Tiny lollies walking around
Jelly beans sleeping on the ground
KitKat crunching around
Milky Bar standing straight in the sky
Mars coming to visit our town
Candyfloss standing as trees
The king wondering where's the sun
Oh no, I think I've eaten lots of sweets.

Gajuri Thevarajah (7)
Yeading Junior School, Hayes

Dragons

D racula dragons on the escape.
R unning on the wild, as red as blood.
A stounding fire coming around.
G ruesome people running around.
O val, golden chrome on the chest.
N asty mayhem going around.
S harp teeth all around.

Banujas Siva (7)
Yeading Junior School, Hayes

Ayaan's Kennings

Mother-lover,
Crisp-liker,
Family-liker,
Job-helper,
Family-helper,
Brother-annoyer,
Sweet-smeller,
Sticker-hater.

Ayaan Jelle (9)
Yeading Junior School, Hayes

Giant Spiders Invade

S pooky spider invade
P eople run away
I am super scared of the 18-legged monster
D on't stand like a melon
E veryone run away
R un, run, run away, we're getting invaded
S pooky spiders are out of this world.

Angelina Ali Pestana (10)
Yeading Junior School, Hayes

Lema's School

She had a light brown, smooth hairy body
There was a rude, mean angry teacher
There were strange pencils
And the school bus had five rooms filled with lots of seats
In each room they sat on soft cushions
All their books were black
But our books were rainbow coloured.

Fatema Mirza (7)
Yeading Junior School, Hayes

Bright Light

Resting near the moon
But invisible at noon.
People counting on Friday
Then trying on Monday.
Trying to be visible at noon
To be the next bright light.

Ally Mohammed (10)
Yeading Junior School, Hayes

YOUNG WRITERS INFORMATION

We hope you have enjoyed reading this book – and that you will continue to in the coming years.

If you're a young writer who enjoys reading and creative writing, or the parent of an enthusiastic poet or story writer, do visit our website www.youngwriters.co.uk. Here you will find free competitions, workshops and games, as well as recommended reads, a poetry glossary and our blog.

If you would like to order further copies of this book, or any of our other titles give us a call or visit **www.youngwriters.co.uk.**

Young Writers
Remus House
Coltsfoot Drive
Peterborough
PE2 9BF

(01733) 890066 / 898110
info@youngwriters.co.uk

A World About Sweets

S tream of strawberry cream
W illy Wonka swims in the water
E lephant-eating insects
E yes with jelly elephants
T ofu and yummy candy.

Ilma Gouse (7)
Yeading Junior School, Hayes

Sweet World

Sweet candy
Brown gingerbread houses
Eating delicious chocolate
Eating sweet candy
Terrific frame of chocolate sweets.

Nemat Malik (7)
Yeading Junior School, Hayes

Stars

S parkling through the night
T hey're mint, golden suns
A cross the night they guide us
R unning through the huge space
S hining through this universe.

Mohammed Ali (7)
Yeading Junior School, Hayes